T0320568

Online Social Networks Security

Online Social Networks Security

Principles, Algorithm, Applications, and Perspectives

Brij B. Gupta & Somya Ranjan Sahoo

CRC Press
Taylor & Francis Group
Boca Raton London New York

CRC Press is an imprint of the
Taylor & Francis Group, an **informa** business

First edition published 2021

by CRC Press
6000 Broken Sound Parkway NW, Suite 300, Boca Raton, FL 33487-2742

and by CRC Press
2 Park Square, Milton Park, Abingdon, Oxon, OX14 4RN

© 2021 Taylor & Francis Group, LLC

CRC Press is an imprint of Taylor & Francis Group, LLC

ISBN: 9780367619794 (hbk)
ISBN: 9781003107378 (ebk)

Typeset in Times
by KnowledgeWorks Global Ltd.

Dedicated to my parents and family for their constant support during the course of this book

—B. B. Gupta

Dedicated to my parents, family, and my mentor for their splendid guidance and motivation throughout the journey to the completion of this book.

—Somya Ranjan Sahoo

Contents

Preface   xi
Acknowledgements   xiii
About the Authors   xv

1 Overview of OSNs and Their Impacts on Users   **1**
  1.1 Online Social Network Vulnerabilities   1
    1.1.1 Fundamentals of Online Social Networks   2
  1.2 Functional Parameters of Online Social Network   3
  1.3 Interaction Among Service Providers and Its Users   4
  1.4 Background and Motivation   4
  1.5 Statistical Analysis Based on Usage and Others   6
  1.6 Various Categories of Online Social Networks   9
  1.7 Rapid Growth of Social Network Environment   11
  1.8 Usage of Online Social Networks Based on Requirement   11
  1.9 Online Social Network Issues and Impact   13
  1.10 Difficulties in Detection and Mitigation of Various
     Attacks Against OSNs   14
  1.11 Chapter Summary   16
  References   16

**2 Security Challenges in Social Networking: Taxonomy,
Statistics, and Opportunities**   **19**
  2.1 The Dark Side of Online Social Networks and Media   19
  2.2 Mistakes and Wrong Responses by the People   20
  2.3 Once It's Out: It's Out   20
  2.4 Various Opportunities in OSNs   20
  2.5 Taxonomy of OSN-Based Attacks   21
    2.5.1 Advanced Persistent Threats   21
    2.5.2 Classical Threats   24
    2.5.3 Social Threats   26
  2.6 Taxonomy of Various Solutions Against OSN Attacks   28
    2.6.1 In-Built Security Solution   28
    2.6.2 Third-Party Software Solutions   28
    2.6.3 Other Security Solutions Against OSN Attacks   31
  2.7 Chapter Summary   38
  References   38

3   Fundamentals of Online Social Networks (OSNs) and Opportunities   **45**
3.1   Opportunities in Social Media   45
3.2   Branding   46
3.3   Building of Social Authority in Social Platform   47
3.4   Customers' Engagement   48
3.5   Sending the Word Out   48
3.6   What to Say? and What Not to?   49
3.7   Cobras (Consumer Brand-Related Activity)   50
3.8   Hashtag   51
3.9   Mistake in Replying to Users of Social Network   51
3.10   Collective Intelligence   52
3.11   Conclusion   54
References   54

4   Machine-Learning and Deep-Learning-Based Security Solutions for Detecting Various Attacks on OSNs   **57**
4.1   Introduction   57
4.2   Motivation Towards Working   59
4.3   Problem Definition   59
4.4   Proposed Approach for Fake-Account Detection   59
4.5   Characteristics Analysis of Twitter Accounts   60
4.6   Selection of Features and Computing Feature Sets   60
4.7   Construction of a Raw Dataset and the Creation of a Labelled Dataset from Raw Data   63
4.8   Petri Net-Based Analyser   63
4.9   Simulation of Petri Net in PN2 Environment   64
4.10   Verification Using SPIN Model Checker   65
4.11   Evaluation of Result and Performance Analysis   66
         4.11.1   Execution Method and Result   66
4.12   Chapter Summary   67
References   68

5   Various Threats and Threat-Handling Tools   **71**
5.1   Introduction   71
5.2   Why Attackers Love Social Media Platforms   72
5.3   Categories of Social Media Attacks Based on Account Types 76
         5.3.1   Categories of Online Social Media Attacks   76
5.4   Cyber Security Tools for Protecting User Account and Information   78
5.5   Chapter Summary   80
References   81

6 Preventive Measures and General Practices   **83**
   6.1 Introduction   83
   6.2 Practice Tips to Protect Your System, Account,
       and Information   84
   6.3 Open Issues and Challenges in Existing Security
       Solutions   85
   6.4 Principles to Protect the User Account
       on a Social Platform   87
   6.5 Chapter Summary   91
   References   92

7 Data Theft in Indonesia: A Case Study on Facebook   **95**
   7.1 Introduction   95
   7.2 Facebook Data Breaker in Indonesia   97
       7.2.1 Expert Opinion Regarding the Data Leak Case   97
       7.2.2 NGO Comments on the Privacy Issues   98
       7.2.3 Government Undertook Measures   99
   7.3 Violating of Rights to Privacy (Singapore Case
       Related to Facebook)   99
   7.4 Data Protection Based on International and
       National Law   100
       7.4.1 International Law Instrument—Based Evolution
            of Protection of Privacy Rights   100
   7.5 Conclusion   101
   References   102

Index   103

Preface

In recent years, people have started using virtual meeting environments in everyday lives with the help of global online social networks (OSNs) to facilitate communication. These networks help users to find new friends and build links all over the world. Moreover, sharing of information and thoughts is an important feature of OSNs. Users can share photos, recent activities, videos, interests, applications, and much more with the help of the OSN. The rate of using OSN has increased rapidly in the recent years. OSNs like Google+; Facebook; Twitter; LinkedIn; Sina Weibo; VKontakte; and Mixi, a Japanese social network, have become the preferred way to communicate for billions of daily active users. Users spend a lot of time to update their content, communicate with early users, and browse other accounts to find information, which is the main purpose of social networking websites. OSN can eliminate the geographical and economical barriers between the users for communication and information sharing. Due to this, it has become a fascinating test bed for numerous cyberattacks comprising Cross-Site Scripting, SQL injection, DDoS, phishing, spamming, fake profile, spammer, etc. This book elaborates on the various attacks with their classification, countermeasures, and consequences. It also highlights some key contributions related to current defensive approaches to various types of attacks on OSNs. Moreover, it represents machine learning and deep-learning-based approaches to mitigate various types of attacks on OSNs. Finally, this book highlights some case studies related to cyberattacks in Facebook. Specifically, the chapters contained in this book are summarized as follows:

Chapter 1: Overview of OSNs and Their Impact on Users. This chapter primarily focuses on the various types of security issues and vulnerabilities exploited by data snoopers to launch various types of attacks against social network users.

Chapter 2: Security Challenges in Online Social Networking: Taxonomies, Statistics and Opportunities. This chapter provides a classification of various security attacks specific to the social network platforms. It also highlights statistics depicting the usage of social media among Internet users, percentage of attacks in various scenarios, and so on.

Chapter 3: Fundamentals of Online Social Networks (OSNs) and Opportunities. This chapter provides deep insight into attacks on OSNs, their classification, scenarios of OSN attacks, and various consequences of OSN attacks. Furthermore, it describes existing defensive methodologies against OSN attack with their strengths and weaknesses. It also provides a comparative study of all these techniques.

Chapter 4: Machine Learning and Deep-learning-based Security Solutions for Detecting Various Attacks on OSNs. This chapter discusses various challenges in the existing state-of-the-art techniques. Later on, it also elaborates on an efficient and robust mechanism to detect various threats in OSN platforms. The chapter also discusses about strengths and limitations on OSNs.

Chapter 5: Various Threats and Threat-Handling Tools. This chapter discusses types of OSN threats that can have severe impact on social actors. Moreover, it also describes different types of tools that aid in detecting and mitigating various threats.

Chapter 6: Preventive Measures and General Practices. This chapter discusses the general methods and practices that can be applied in the development level of browser or web applications, or both, to safeguard against various attacks in OSN. It also illuminates the path for future research directions by highlighting the existing issues in currently available solutions.

Chapter 7: Data Theft in Indonesia: A Case Study on Facebook. This chapter describes one of the case studies on Facebook related to data theft in Indonesia. It highlights different scenarios of cyberattacks and the preventive measures that can be taken through various legal actions by the government.

Acknowledgements

We take this precious opportunity to express our deep sense of gratitude to those who are directly or indirectly associated with this book. We are also thankful to our friends and colleagues for their support, encouragement, and valuable time that they spared for discussing various micro-level aspects related to this book. Moreover, we would like to thank CRC Press, Taylor & Francis Group editor Ms Gabriella Williams and her team for their consistent support and cooperation throughout the development of this book. Furthermore, this book would not have been possible without the unconditional love, constant inspiration, and passionate encouragement from our parents, family members, and relatives. Finally, we would like to express our gratitude to God by bowing our heads for lavishing on us continuous blessings and the enthusiasm to complete this book.

B. B. Gupta
Somya Ranjan Sahoo

About the Authors

B. B. Gupta received his PhD in information and cyber security from Indian Institute of Technology, Roorkee, India. He has published more than 250 research papers in international journals and conferences of high repute and has visited several countries like Canada, Japan, the United states, the United Kingdom, Malaysia, Australia, Thailand, China, Hong Kong, Italy, Spain, etc. to present his research work. His biography was published in the 30th edition of *Marquis Who's Who in the World*, 2012. Dr. Gupta also received the Young Faculty Research Fellowship award from the Ministry of Electronics and Information Technology, Government of India, in 2018. He is the principal investigator for various R&D projects. He serves or has served as associate editor of *IEEE Access, IEEE TII, FGCS, IJICS, IJCSE, ACM TOIT,* and *ASOC*, among other journals. At present, Dr. Gupta is an assistant professor in the Department of Computer Engineering, National Institute of Technology, Kurukshetra, India. His research interests include information security, cyber security, mobile security, cloud computing, web security, intrusion detection, and phishing.

Somya Ranjan Sahoo is currently pursuing his PhD in information and cyber security from National Institute of Technology (NIT), Kurukshetra, India. He has completed his M. Tech. in data mining from Bijupatnayak University of Technology (BPUT), Rourkela, India and his B. Tech. in information technology from Silicon Institute of Technology, Bhubaneswar, India. His research interests include online social network security, big data analysis and security, database security and cyber security, and Internet of Things security. He has published a number of research papers with various reputable publishers, like Elsevier, Taylor & Francis, and Inderscience.

Overview of OSNs and Their Impacts on Users

1

In recent years we have seen more and more individuals use virtual meeting places and platforms in their daily lives, known as online social networks (OSNs). To keep contact worldwide, these networks help the user a lot with new friends. Sharing of personal information is one of the significant applications of OSN; however, users also share other information such as images, various activities, videos, and concerns on OSN platforms. OSNs like Google+ (Google+), Facebook, TikTok, Twitter, LinkedIn, are a favoured way of communication for billions of daily active users. Users spend maximum time in communicating with other profiles, and updating their accounts and browsing others' profiles, which is the main implication of OSNs. Personal information shared on these networks is up-to-date due to the frequent activity by users and, thereby, lures the attackers. Therefore, this chapter focuses on providing a thorough account of the most obvious and treacherous vulnerabilities that are affecting the social network platforms and user credentials worldwide. Furthermore, the authors have summarised the related statistics report from various trusted sources. It highlights the security threats corresponding to different social network services. Finally, a comprehensive assessment of the vulnerabilities has been provided with respect to the identified risk path rating method.

1.1 ONLINE SOCIAL NETWORK VULNERABILITIES

In current scenario, OSN is one of the most perilous security threats to the society and mankind. According to the recent study by various security development firms such as McAfee and Norton, more than 1.5 billion people on a reputable social network platform such as Facebook alone, will be a major threat over the year. The huge load of information disclosed by different users helps the hackers to conduct malicious activities over the Internet. All this information indirectly exposes more useful data about the users, even though the user did not share. Thus, it can violate the user's privacy (Sahoo & Gupta, 2020). If involved in a serious crime, this information could help adversaries. Therefore, OSNs such as Twitter does not permit the users to furnish significant private information, but adversaries can spoof the user's posts and thereby find what they need. For example, different companies can use user's private information to show online advertisements to a user's profile on the basis of his/her thoughts (Tucker, 2010), to gain useful perceptivity. A recent statistic by McAfee has shown that more than 70% of organisations faced security breaches from various social network platforms. To mitigate various risks, all vulnerabilities related to social media, including fake profiles (Agrawal, Wang, Sahoo, & Gupta, 2019), identity theft, phishing attack (Sahoo & Gupta, 2019), and twin attack, should be considered.

1.1.1 Fundamentals of Online Social Networks

OSN services are "web-based services that allow individuals to construct a public or semi-public profile within a bounded system" (Woungang et al., 2018), articulate a list of other users with whom they share a connection, and view and traverse their list of connections and those made by others within the system. Particularly, sharing of information through direct communication; instant messaging; and profile annotation using comments, recommendations, and text with some links to redirect other profiles, e.g. picture tagging and photo tagging, are the various usages of OSNs. All these contexts are used for publications and browsing of multimedia content over social platforms. In addition, OSNs support some third-party applications for interaction among users and enhance other facilities of OSNs from poking to likeness with other members. Various services are offered by social network service providers like Google+, Facebook, Twitter, LinkedIn, Sina Weibo, and VKontakte. These have become the favoured way of information sharing for billions of users. In general, a variety of content is stored and shared by the user over social platform. All these contents are stored at service provider's database under its control, especially to protect the content from various types of attacks. All this information is publicly visible or, if the users are concerned about security, they use the principle of security setting to protect their content (Dorgham, Al-Rahamneh, Almomani, & Khatatneh, 2018; Ouaguid, Abghour, & Ouzzif, 2018; Zhu & Han, 2018).

1.2 FUNCTIONAL PARAMETERS OF ONLINE SOCIAL NETWORK

Different OSNs are usually tailored for some specific uses, but the functionality of these networks is quite standardised. In general, the functionality of OSNs can be classified into three main categories:

- *Networking function*: It is the actual work of OSN, i.e. to build a social relationship between users within a virtual platform by eliminating geographical barriers. In particular, it provides the facility of building and maintaining the social network structure. OSN users build their profiles by adding other accounts and establishing their networks through sharing and interaction of information among users. To create their accounts, users use the create function option by putting their personal details on the OSN platform. The users then establish their networks by profile lookup features. Thereafter, the users use various features of OSNs to communicate, share, and interact with others in the network.

- *Data function*: The users on different OSNs advertise themselves by posting blogs, conducting forums, creating polls, chatting, direct messaging, and liking and sharing different posts, etc. Features like profile update help the user to update their account and maintain the same by providing latest information to their friends. Using post function, users communicate and share their contents on social platform to show their interest and invite other users to visit their profiles. This information is not only textual but also contains videos, audios, links, etc. A user also uses the facility of OSN database to store personal information by transferring digital contents. Also, to rate other users' content on social platform, user uses "like" and "dislike" function.

- *Access control function*: To define the user's own account privacy, access control mechanisms are provided by the service provider in OSNs. In particular, OSN users may have control over their visibility or online presence, contacts, profile information, and uploaded contents. All this information is uploaded on OSN, and the list of profiles have the permission to access it. The known profiles are registered with user groups such as friends, mutual friends, or some other groups such as school friends and family, etc.

1.3 INTERACTION AMONG SERVICE PROVIDERS AND ITS USERS

OSN service providers provide various social networking services and some additional interfaces to their users for information sharing, interaction, and content sharing with other users on the same social network platform. These users are from various domains to pursue their goals. OSN users may advertise their services and products through OSN. These advertisements are of different kinds such as commercial products, marketing products, and other services. Another type of users in OSNs are known as the third-party service providers, who use OSN services to extend their service and develop new applications. These applications include games and quizzes, executed through server control of third-party services via their application programming interfaces (APIs). Also, these applications have extensive access to users' private information on OSNs. Finally, the users act as a data analyst in OSNs. These users have the authenticity to access the personal profile of different users and publicise information in the form of texts, audios, videos, and links. The activities between service providers, user, and third-party developer act as a cyclic process for communication and interaction. The detail of communication and connection between social network service providers and the users is depicted in Figure 1.1.

1.4 BACKGROUND AND MOTIVATION

When the use of the Internet became widespread, people experienced a whole new paradigm. Moreover, personal lifestyle also transformed due to the emergence of new devices and systems. An OSN has become an essential part of human life – starting from sharing of private content such as age, date of birth, bank account number, address, pictures, text messages, sharing latest news to sharing news-related information (Rathore, Sharma, Loia, Jeong, & Park, 2017). Other activities include sharing exam question papers, student assignments, workshop details, various online surveys, marketing information, targeting customers in business domain, jokes, songs, and videos by the users over OSNs (Zeidanloo, Zadeh, Shooshtari, Safari, & Zamani, 2010). Also, every year the number of OSN users has been enhancing rapidly worldwide. According to the Statista statistics report (Statista Report about Online Social Networking Users, n.d.), the number of OSN users worldwide from 2010 to 2020 and forecast up to 2023 are depicted in Figure 1.2. Also, this report

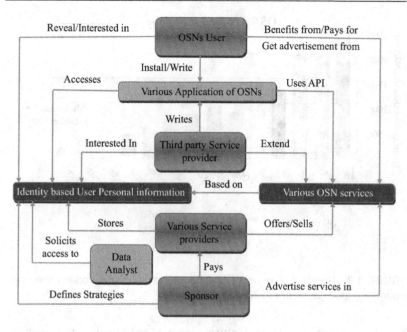

FIGURE 1.1 Communication and connection between social network provider and its user.

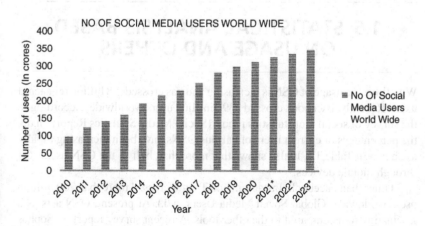

FIGURE 1.2 Number of online social network users worldwide from 2010 to 2020 and forecast up to 2023.

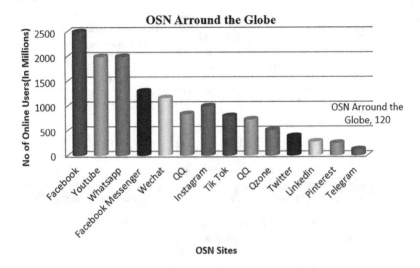

FIGURE 1.3 Number of users of leading online social networking websites around the globe as of July 2020.

describes the statistics of leading OSNs as on July 2020 (Statista Report about Online Social Networking Users, n.d.) on the basis of the number of current users on different OSNs as depicted in Figure 1.3. It is stated that Facebook is the leading OSN globally.

1.5 STATISTICAL ANALYSIS BASED ON USAGE AND OTHERS

With time, the usage of OSN is increasing and has crossed 2.8 billion registered users. Recently, Facebook crossed 2396 million users worldwide. According to the survey of social plot statistics report (Social Media Statistics Report., n.d.), the percentages of current users of various OSNs have been increasing rapidly as shown in Table 1.1. It also shows that more than half of the OSN users surf through mobile devices.

Other than Facebook, Instagram and Twitter crossed more than 700 million users worldwide (Global Social Media Users, n.d.). At present, OSN acts as a fascinating tool compared to the other tools. A recent survey report by Sophos revealed that 100% users of United Arab Emirates use social networking sites, a spectacular increase from few surveys in the past as depicted in Figure 1.4.

TABLE 1.1 Number of daily, monthly, total, and active mobile OSN users

| | STATISTICS | | | |
OSN WEBSITE	NUMBER OF USERS AS COMPARED TO INTERNET USERS	MONTHLY ACTIVE OSN USERS	DAILY ACTIVE USERS	DAILY ACTIVE MOBILE USERS
Facebook	79%	1.79 billion	1.18 billion	1.09 billion
Twitter	24%	317 million	100 million	82% of total active users
LinkedIn	29%	106 million	40%	41% of total active users
Instagram	32%	500 million	60%	15%
Google+	540 million	335 million	22%	18%
Pinterest Statistics	31%	100 million	More than 30%	25% of total active users
Snapchat	More than 40%	200 million	150 million	38% of total active users

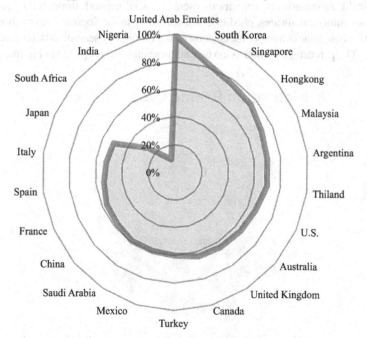

The utilization of OSN for various country

FIGURE 1.4 Percentage of population that uses OSNs worldwide as on July 2020.

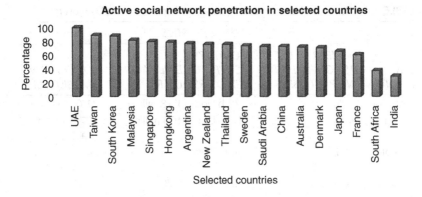

FIGURE 1.5 Social network penetration in different regions around the globe as on July 2020.

Figure 1.5 shows Internet usage through social media in various regions of the world. Adversaries attack various users on social network through fake profiles, spammers, malwares, phishing, etc., according to the Sophos security threat report. These attacks hamper users' content and account by sending different messages. The percentage of motivation behind these attacks is depicted in Figure 1.6.

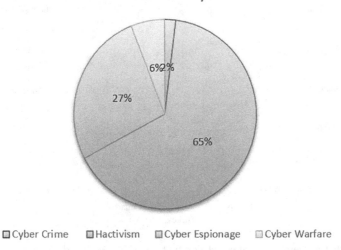

FIGURE 1.6 Percentage of motivation behind cyberattacks.

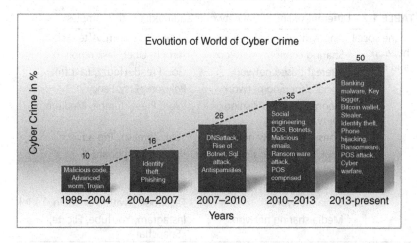

FIGURE 1.7 Evolution of world of cyber-crime from 1998 to present.

Also, most of the surveys reveal that, among all users, around 70% users are teenagers and round 10–20% of them are in the age group of 10–18 years. According to InfoSec institute threat report, the various attacks on OSN gradually changed from 1998 with malicious code, Trojan, and it will spread to high-profile attacks and threats described in Figure 1.7. In current scenario, attackers try to capture the user's credential through various applications as well as message services.

1.6 VARIOUS CATEGORIES OF ONLINE SOCIAL NETWORKS

In recent times, people have always been looking for different ways of communication and information sharing. In this age of digitisation, people have developed various social networking platforms and apps to be socially active on the Internet. Based on the application, the different social networks and media are categorised into different groups as depicted in Table 1.2.

- *Anonymous social media (ASM)*: Anonymously sharing of information and content on OSNs through mobile and web-based platform is a subcategory of various social media. Another prominent factor of ASM/network is that the posted information is not connected with any particular identity or profile users.

TABLE 1.2   Different online social networks and media with examples

Online social network and media	Anonymous social network	Whisper, Ask.fm, After School
	Sharing economy network	Airbnb, Uber, Task rabbit
	Interest-based network	Good read, Houzz, Last.fm
	Social shopping network	Polyvore, Etsy, Fancy
	Blogging and publishing network	Word Press, Tumblr, Medium
	Consumer review network	Yelp, Zomato, Trip advisor
	Book marking and curation network	Pinterest, Flipboard
	Discussion forum	Reddit, Quora, Digg
	Social networks	Facebook, Twitter, LinkedIn, TikTok
	Media sharing network	Instagram, YouTube, Flicate, Snapchat

- *Sharing economy network*: This network is also known as a collaborative or peer-to-peer network-based sharing concept, highlighting the ability and individual performance to rent or borrow goods rather than buying or owning them.
- *Interest-based networks*: Interest-based social networks behave like other social networks built with the interest of bringing audience groups together. To get the benefit, interest-based networks take help of other social network services to share their product, travel details, food, and fashion. There are certain platforms, where they allow the users to hide their details. This helps the users to share their problems and hardships without disclosing personal information.
- *Social shopping network*: Social shopping is one of the e-commerce methods where users perform different transactions for buying or selling different products and may also share their experiences or reviews with other users. Examples are Flipkart, Amazon, and eBay.
- *Blogging and publishing network*: A blog is a way to express thoughts, demonstrate their presence, and provide different contents to Internet users. Most of the time, it behaves as a software service that is used to publish users' content in the form of a blog on World Wide Web compared to websites.
- *Consumer review network*: It is a platform to review products and services received by the customers, who purchased that product/service, in the form of a feedback on shopping websites and electronic commerce.
- *Bookmarking and content curation networks*: One method of curation is called social bookmarking. The social bookmarking network in particular lacks the ability for the curator to add significant

information, content, and commentary. It also has the facility to organise the content for the curator.

- *Discussion forum*: Forum is one of the online discussion platforms where users like students and professionals discuss their queries and get answers from others. It behaves like a platform for content sharing by the users based on their interest.
- *Social networks*: A social networking service is one of the online platforms to build social relation between peoples by eliminating geographical barriers while having interest professionally and personally.
- *Media sharing network*: These are website that enable users to store, share, and post multimedia files with other users. Such a network is often premium based, providing some free space for storage.

1.7 RAPID GROWTH OF SOCIAL NETWORK ENVIRONMENT

The increasing number of users on OSNs invites attackers to engage in some malicious activities. Based on the analysis of (Facebook DAU) Zophoria Statistics Report (n.d.), the average number of users who login into Facebook as daily active users is 1.427 billion as of July 2019, which represents 17% rise every year. The increasing use of OSNs in mobile devices has lead to high security issues. As per the analysis of global social media statistics (Global Social Media Users, n.d.), users between 16 and 44 years of age have used OSNs over the past months. In Japan, girls between 10 and 19 years of age have a Twitter account and the percentage is higher than 80% according to the statistics report by e-marketer (Chen et al., 2013). Among all the Internet users, more than 50% are teenagers who use Facebook for their communication (Statista Report about Online Social Networking Users, n.d.). However, the increasing popularity creates a big challenge to protect user account as well as their personal information from attackers.

1.8 USAGE OF ONLINE SOCIAL NETWORKS BASED ON REQUIREMENT

Currently, the usage of OSN is increasing rapidly day by day and has crossed 2.5 billion active users. Among all these OSNs, Facebook has more than 50% users worldwide. Other than this, Instagram has 1000 million, Twitter has more than 500 million, and LinkedIn has 106 million users worldwide (Global Social Media Users, n.d.). According to the current survey report by Sophos, 100% users of United Arab Emirates use OSN sites, a gradual rise from past few surveys. According to various surveys, more than 50% of the OSN users are adolescents. Moreover, the statistics report also reveals that around 10–20% recorded users are between the ages of 10 and 18. Particularly on Facebook, the time spent by the user is tremendous. Based on the statistics report by World Statista statistics (Statista Report about Online Social Networking Users, n.d.), more than one-fourth of the world's population uses Facebook for information exchange (Facebook, n.d.). The use of Facebook as social network platform increased exponentially from the year 2010 to 2020, i.e. more than 750%. Another report by Zephoria statistics (Zophoria Statistics Report, n.d.) says that the average number of daily active users who log onto Facebook is 1.427 billion as up to the last quarter of 2020, which shows a 17% steps-up in every year. Day by day, the rapid increasing use of OSN with mobile has led to high security issues.

According to the report by Global Social Media statistics (Global Social Media Users, n.d.), users aged between 16 and 44 years use OSNs, which is more than 95% of total users. In the current scenario, professional's report says that Twitter is a more secure platform as compared to other OSNs. With the help of various OSN services, industrial fabricators can be more close to their customers by publishing various informative links to their sites, photos of various products, etc. Social networking services such as Facebook and Twitter provide the following benefits to industrial manufacturer:

- *Enhance commitment and trademark*: To broadcast content in OSN related to product, business, and services is a great way. If a particular product is liked by a follower, they may share the information with their contact list or friends to increase customer loyalty and relation.
- *Increase customer insights*: To collect feedback and new ideas, the developer interacts directly with the customers and enquires about the various features they would like.
- *Make an agenda and post consistently*: The follower always wants more from developer sites related to the product on regular basis. So, it is very essential to create an agenda related to that product and update the same based on demand.
- *Apply OSN handling tools*: To save time, OSN management tools help the customer to maintain regular posting schedules of various products as advertisement. It also helps to publish content across various platforms, cooperate with team members, and track the product results.

1.9 ONLINE SOCIAL NETWORK ISSUES AND IMPACT

Sharing of valuable content in the form of audios, videos, images, location updates, personal and professional information; tagging; and blogging have been the daily activities of social network users. All this information attracts various issues towards web and its users. These issues are categorised into various groups based on their usage and behaviour:

- *Safety of mankind*: Due to high user activity in social network platform, online threats are easily exposed by users such as online predator, fraud, identity theft, and various cybercriminal attacks. Various reports generated by different security analysts state that OSN platform is the most common medium for various attacks. Sharing confidential information like bank account details, credit card information, and location updates are the main gateway of identity theft attack. Due to the public information shared, it summonses the attacker to do supplementary activities on the OSN. Similar to identity theft attack, sphere phishing attack captures user's financial information to do some malicious activity over the net.
- *Profiling issues*: This process is a subroutine to create an account and do some malicious activities. To create individual accounts, people gather information from various sources and use the same. According to the recent study on different OSNs, Facebook and MySpace were collectively responsible for more than 80% of ads. The statistics stated before confirmed that a seller is keen to utilise hastily the increasing demand of OSNs for advertising and promoting their goods and services. Different online advertising agencies are Ogilvy and Mather, IDEO, Leo Burnett, Sid Lee, etc.
- *Reputation-related issues*: It is a common behavior of the community towards social network users or a group. It plays a big role in various fields like an organisation, social status, and various social online groups. For sharing information publicly with known and unknowns, various people rely on social networking services. Due to these services, the social reputation of the user degrades. Users spread offensive blogs and often post on social platforms to collect user credentials. Through advertising, corporates market their

products and services through different users. Also, for updating personal information, various social network services are used. In addition, OSN not only regulates the condition of its user but also creates a big fuss for them.

1.10 DIFFICULTIES IN DETECTION AND MITIGATION OF VARIOUS ATTACKS AGAINST OSNs

Due to the various technical complications, the detection and mitigation of various threats in social network platforms have become difficult. Some of the complications are described below:

- *Privacy problems and alarms*: Various service providers provide different privacy and security settings to different users for their account protection. We have detected various privacy mechanisms provided by OSNs for securing the accounts. There could be a wide range of discrimination that endures in OSN privacy. It has been noted that many of the OSN users are not aware of the privacy settings (Fang & LeFevre, 2010). Some of the features related to privacy settings on OSNs are depicted in Table 1.3.
- *Guessing the behaviour of OSN users*: The behaviour of different OSN users varies based on their usage and the features provided by the service provider. Li (2012) describes the regard in which users

TABLE 1.3 Various privacy settings on online social networks

VARIOUS PRIVACY OPTIONS FOR OSN USERS	FACEBOOK	TWITTER	LINKEDIN	GOOGLE+
Visibility mode (active user visibility)	Yes	No	No	No
Medium by which another user finds you	Yes	Yes	Yes	No
Blocking account images	Yes	No	No	Yes
Login alerts	Yes	No	No	Yes
Blocking of spam user	Yes	Yes	Yes	Yes
Message control system	Yes	No	Yes	Yes

hold different OSNs with respect to privacy concerns. As a sample, 250 understudies were chosen randomly from different social network sites and 185 polls are filled effectively. Out of all the content, three-fourths of respondents are male account holders and one-fourth are female. Subsequently, more than 75% of male users are below the age of 40 years. All most all users are using Facebook, and around 45% users are using Twitter for message sharing and information broadcast. Based on the user's behaviour, the personality of the user is predicted. Also, the use of text and style describes the user's behaviour.

- *Different threats in OSNs*: Nowadays, various security issues exist in social network platform based on privacy. It is a challenging task for security analysts and the researchers to protect the user contents and their accounts from various threats. These threats are broadly classified into various groups such as active attacks, passive attacks, and privacy breaches. All these attacks exploit various functionalities provided by social network platform.

- *Security setting on the user's side*: To protect user account and their information in social network platform, security setting is one of the major concerns by the user. Different OSNs like Facebook and Twitter limit protections as a default setting. It is highly crucial for all users to go through their profile security options and set their protection choices as per their uses. By improving the security setting, users on Facebook can limit their account access. However, all these features are not sufficient to protect user's information and accounts from various threats.

- *Lack of security solutions at developers end*: Deployment of total security solution is not possible by the developer team of social networks due to public access. In addition, such developers focus mainly on the development of products and their compatibility with the users.

- *Maintaining QoS during attack*: During various attacks on OSNs, the resources are exhausted and legitimate user's quality of service (QoS) degrades based on the uses (Liu et al., 2017). Hence, it is a big challenge to maintain the desired QoS for every user over the OSN.

- *High false-positive rate with low detection*: Reducing the impact of attack, detection, and mitigation of various threats in OSNs requires timely detection (Freeman, 2017). Faster detection mechanism may lead to an increase in the misclassification rate and vice versa. Hence, it is required to detect the threats quickly with high detection and less false-positive rate.

1.11 CHAPTER SUMMARY

For communication and information sharing, OSN is a prominent gateway for people nowadays. The users of the OSNs enjoy a lot while using social network platforms. This leads to attracting various attackers to engage in some malicious activities. Therefore, the main focus of this chapter is to describe the rapid growth of OSNs in different domains. It also illuminates various statistics unveiled by different security organisations. This chapter also provides a comprehensive detail regarding the various usages of OSNs based on different requirements and some of the harmful vulnerabilities. It concludes that there are some security issues in various OSN domains which hamper user credentials and reputation. Furthermore, this chapter describes some difficulties related to the detection and mitigation of various attacks against OSNs.

REFERENCES

Chen, C., Wu, K., Srinivasan, V., & Zhang, X. (2013, August). Battling the internet water army: Detection of hidden paid posters. In 2013 IEEE/ACM International Conference on Advances in Social Networks Analysis and Mining (ASONAM 2013) (pp. 116–120). IEEE.

Dorgham, O., Al-Rahamneh, B., Almomani, A., & Khatatneh, K. F. (2018). Enhancing the security of exchanging and storing DICOM medical images on the cloud. *International Journal of Cloud Applications and Computing (IJCAC)*, 8(1), 154–172.

Facebook. (n.d.). https://www.facebook.com/

Fang, L., & LeFevre, K. (2010). *Privacy wizards for social networking sites* (p. 351). https://doi.org/10.1145/1772690.1772727

Freeman, D. M. (2017). Can you spot the fakes? On the limitations of user feedback in online social networks. In *26th International World Wide Web Conference, WWW 2017*, 1093–1102. https://doi.org/10.1145/3038912.3052706

Global Social Media Users. (n.d.). http://www.smartinsights.com/social-media-marketing/social-media-strategy/new-global-social-media-research/

Google+ Available At. (n.d.). https://plus.google.com

Campos, S. B. Jr, Tavares, G. F. C., Igawa, G. M., & Guido, M. L. P. Jr, R. C. (2018). Detection of human, legitimate bot, and malicious bot in online social networks based on wavelets. *ACM Transactions on Multimedia Computing, Communications, and Applications*, 14(1s), 1–17. https://doi.org/10.1145/3183506

Li, Y. (2012). Theories in online information privacy research: A critical review and an integrated framework. *Decision Support Systems*, 54(1), 471–481.

LinkedIn. (n.d.). https://in.linkedin.com/

Liu, P., Xu, Z., Ai, J., & Wang, F. (2017). Identifying indicators of fake reviews based on spammer's behavior features. In *Proceedings – 2017 IEEE International Conference on Software Quality, Reliability and Security Companion, QRS-C 2017, 61502299,* 396–403. https://doi.org/10.1109/QRS-C.2017.72

Ouaguid, A., Abghour, N., & Ouzzif, M. (2018). A novel security framework for managing android permissions using blockchain technology. *International Journal of Cloud Applications and Computing (IJCAC), 8*(1), 55–79.

Rathore, S., Sharma, P. K., Loia, V., Jeong, Y. S., & Park, J. H. (2017). Social network security: Issues, challenges, threats, and solutions. *Information Sciences, 421* 43–69. https://doi.org/10.1016/j.ins.2017.08.063

Sahoo, S. R., & Gupta, B. B. (2018). Security Issues and Challenges in Online Social Networks (OSNs) Based on User Perspective. *Computer and Cyber Security,* 591–606.

Sahoo, S. R., & Gupta, B. B. (2019). Classification of various attacks and their defence mechanism in online social networks: A survey. *Enterprise Information Systems, 00*(00), 1–33. doi: https://doi.org/10.1080/17517575.2019.1605542.

Sahoo, S. R., & Gupta., B. B. (2020). Classification of spammer and nonspammer content in online social network using genetic algorithm-based feature selection. *Enterprise Information Systems, 14*(5), 710–736. https://doi.org/10.1080/175175 75.2020.1712742

Social Media Statistics Report. (n.d.). https://socialpilot.co/blog/151-amazing-social-media-statistics-know-2018.

Statista Report about Online Social Networking Users. (n.d.). https://www.statista.com/statistics/278414/number-of-worldwide-social-network-users/

Tucker, C. E. (2010). Social networks, personalized advertising, and privacy controls. *Social Science Research Network, 51*(5), 546–562. doi: https://doi.org/10.2139/ssrn.1694319.

Twitter. (n.d.). https://twitter.com/

Woungang, I., Eds, A. A., Hutchison, D., Marra, F., Gragnaniello, D., Cozzolino, D., Verdoliva, L., … Alfaro, L. De. (2018). Supervised learning for fake News detection. *Proceedings - IEEE 1st Conference on Multimedia Information Processing and Retrieval, MIPR 2018, 4*(1), 76–81. https://doi.org/10.1109/MIS.2019.2899143

Zeidanloo, H. R., Zadeh, M. J., Shooshtari, A., Safari, P. V., & Zamani, M., M. (2010). A taxonomy of botnet detection techniques. *Proceedings – 2010 3rd IEEE International Conference on Computer Science and Information Technology, ICCSIT 2010, 2,* 158–162. https://doi.org/10.1109/ICCSIT.2010.5563555

Zhu, S., & Han, Y. (2018). Secure data outsourcing scheme in cloud computing with attribute-based encryption. *International Journal of High Performance Computing and Networking, 12*(2), 128–136.

Zophoria Statistics Report. (n.d.). https://zephoria.com/top-15-valuable-facebook-statistics/

Security Challenges in Social Networking

2

Taxonomy, Statistics, and Opportunities

This chapter elaborates an overview of online social networks (OSNs) threats, including its various defensive approaches. This chapter also discusses various threats that affect the user's credentials through various ways, including how it propagates through various media. Furthermore, this chapter sheds some light on how the information flows among different parties in OSNs and provides the information related to the usage of OSNs with respect to different regions. Moreover, it discusses the plethora of security attacks on the OSN platform and examines various approaches proposed by different researchers to defend against these attacks.

2.1 THE DARK SIDE OF ONLINE SOCIAL NETWORKS AND MEDIA

The OSNs bring different people into a single platform for sharing information for good, but it also invites supporters of terror, extremism, and hatred (Gupta & Gugulothu, 2018; Gupta, Gupta, & Chaudhary, 2019; Zhang et al.,

2019; Zheng, He, Zhang, Wu, & Ji, 2019). There are numerous examples where online narratives have incited users to commit various violent acts on a social network platform, for example, one of the posts shared by VKontakte on a social network group supporting terrorism activities. And later this led a big impact on preparing to attack the city of Karbala in Iraq.

2.2 MISTAKES AND WRONG RESPONSES BY THE PEOPLE

Sometimes people require some suggestion from different experts regarding their doubts. When the users post some questions in social networks, they may get suitable answers from them. But, sometimes he/she may get some wrong idea that creates a big negative impact on their works. It also may lead to serious danger in their social life. The negative responses are recorded by various attackers who are trying to get some credentials from different users and also attract social network users towards their account.

2.3 ONCE IT'S OUT: IT'S OUT

The statement 'Once it's Out: It's Out' is best suitable for social media platform because of their accessibility and connectivity. Once a user of any social media platforms posts, tweets, or shares any content, at the same moment that is updated in many accounts over network – also, in some cases that content also shared by other users. That information may mislead various users over the network. Sometimes, intentionally intruders spread the original content with some malicious information to degrade the reputation of the user.

2.4 VARIOUS OPPORTUNITIES IN OSNs

The social network users get many opportunities when they use social network platforms such as Facebook, Twitter, and Instagram. All these opportunities include research-oriented contents, problem-solving, marketing, reputation, management, and recommendation systems. The interaction of the user creates a lot of information in the network. That information is used for diverse research works by different researchers. Also, social networks like LinkedIn provide the user various geographic/demographic information about different users. Furthermore, social network platforms provide a convenient way to get social matters to work and communicate collectively on various kinds of issues. By this process, the scientific publication can speed up the venting process a lot.

2.5 TAXONOMY OF OSN-BASED ATTACKS

The various OSN platforms are communication-based software that provides the facility to the registered users to share their thoughts with their friends and others in the same or different networks. All these communications develop large volumes of information which is shared by various social networks users. As users share private and public information on OSNs, therefore, OSN platforms are vulnerable to numerous cyberattacks (Dewan, 2017). Various threats have been discussed in following sections and also depicted in Figure 2.1.

2.5.1 Advanced Persistent Threats

It is a type of threat by which an intruder, or group of intruders, establishes an illicit, long-term presence on a social network in order to steal sensitive information (Siddiqui, Brill, Davis, & Olmsted, 2016). It includes the following types of attack:

- *Spear phishing attack*: In spear phishing attack, the attackers attempt to steal personal information such as account credentials or financial information from a specific victim for malicious reasons (P & T, 2011). This is achieved by accumulating personal details on the victim such as friends, location, and other details.
- *Whaling attack*: This attack targeted to steal personal information from a company such as fiscal content or employee's personal details for malicious reasons (Sadhya & Singh, 2017). This type of attack specifically targets CEO, CFO, CTO, or other executive personals who have complete access to sensitive data and hold position and power in companies. It is called 'whaling' because of the size of the targets relative to those of typical phishing attacks (Al-Zoubi,

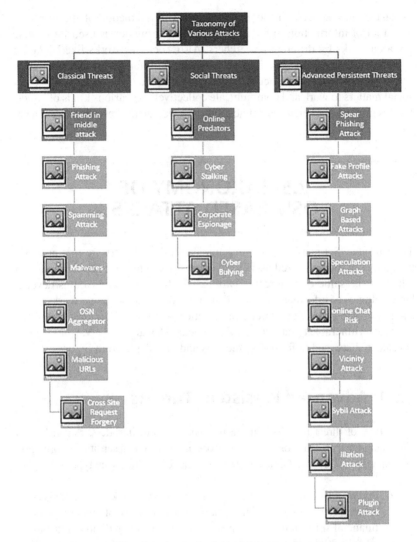

FIGURE 2.1 Taxonomy of various attacks in OSNs based on their behaviour.

Alqatawna, & Faris, 2017). However, this attack is similar to phishing attack.

- *Fake profile attack*: To collect information from unknown users, attackers create a fake profile by collecting some basic information about the user. Also, the adversary creates multiple accounts in different networks. The attack on the basis of fake profile (Sahoo & Gupta, n.d.) is alike to Sybil or social network bots attack (Koll,

Schwarzmaier, Li, Li, & Fu, 2017). The social bot and fake profile user collect private information of the user by requesting other accounts who reply frequently.

- *DDoS attack*: In this attack, the attackers overtake other users' resources by blocking legitimate customers. By this process, attackers use social network platforms to exploit someone conducting powerful DDoS attack. As an example, social networks like Facebook allow users to add tags. When the user uploads image, Facebook crawls images from various external sources and caches it. By using dynamic parameter, Facebook user includes any images repeatedly with dynamic parameters. Later, all these contents are downloaded by Facebook by forced multiple times in single server.
- *Graph-based attack*: Graphical representation of various users in a common platform is treated as social network or OSN. When the contact list of the user increases by storing other users' details, the size of the network structure is enlarged. To search various data content and subject matter on OSN, graph-based search helps the user a lot. The process of searching in graph structure increases the security and privacy issues (Jorquera Valero et al., 2018).
- *Speculation attack*: To protect the identity from unauthorized access, OSN users use anonymisation method. Speculation attack uses various machine learning approaches to gather personal information that are available publicly like intimate preference and religious association (Sahoo & Gupta, 2019b).
- *Online chat risk*: For communication and information sharing with others, OSNs provide online chat feature option. Apart from this service, most of the OSNs provide the facility to communicate with other users through online chat. In addition, other chat services such as Internet Relay Chat, MSN, and ICQ are used by OSN users for direct interaction and information sharing (Palmieri, Fiore, & Castiglione, 2011). During this process, they share their personal information without the fear of information abuse. Taking this advantage, any hackers or attackers access personal information and misuse for malicious purposes.
  - *Vicinity attack*: Sharing of information is the main factor for using OSNs. The information may contain some personal credentials like bank account number, which is sensitive to any individual. To protect the data, anonymisation technique is required before making the data available publicly. If attackers have certain information about victim, they can easily collect the information from neighbours, the victim may be re-identified from the social network if anonymisation technique is used by the victim (Zhang, Zheng, Li, Du, & Zhu, 2014).

- *De-anonymisation attack*: Hiding the personal information by using cryptology techniques to protest against unauthorised access is called anonymisation. In this technique (Ding, Zhang, Wan, & Gu, 2010), attackers identify the network topology using packet tracer tools, user group membership and access cookies to theft user personal information.
- *Sybil attack*: The author describes Sybil attack in Sarode and Mishra (2015). It works mainly on multi-hop systems and distributed environments. By this process, attackers create many fake accounts to collect public and private information of the user. The main reason behind this is to blame other users. This process also reduces user reputation online (Koll et al., 2017). Moreover, by this process, attack promotes their account by voting for it (Campos, Tavares, Igawa, Guido, & R. C., 2018).
- *Illation attacks*: The illation attack described by the author in Mislove, Viswanath, Gummadi, and Druschel (2010). By this attack, the adversary guesses the personal information of the user that is not available publicly. These attacks can be analysed through network structure and friends of targeted users.
- *Plug-in attack*: OSNs permit certain plug-in like flash and silverlight through browsing environment. When the users log in to those specific sites, they automatically redirect the page to some different sites and downloaded malicious content. Due to such plug-ins, it can broadcast or get directed to other sites with various malicious links and invite attacks to conduct some malfunctions on the social networks (Narain, Kumar, & Gupta, 2012).

2.5.2 Classical Threats

Classical threat propagates rapidly and circulates among social network users through the network structure. In most cases, it affects users' credentials and accounts by capturing personal information of the user. When the user unknowingly clicks on those malicious links, it can be spread among multiple users. This process steals users' credentials and behaves likes a legitimate user and also replaces malicious content of the user's home page. It includes the following types of attacks:

- *Friend in middle attacks*: Sometimes the attackers use various spamming techniques to exploit OSN data. Furthermore, they use those information to steal personal information of the user in an automated fashion (Beato, Conti, & Preneel, 2013).

- *Phishing attacks*: In this attack, the attackers use the network as delivery vehicle for malwares. More than 85% of organisations have suffered from phishing attack. Out of all, 30% of phishing emails get opened. The email attachment is one of the easiest ways to deliver malwares. The top five malware vectors within crime are network propagation (10%), software download by malware (10%), various links in email (39%), email attachment (63%), and web drive (61%) to reveal users' personal information phishing attack (Tian, Yuan, & Yu, 2017) compounding social engineering and technical methods group together to win over other users. All these can be carried out through email spoofing and instant messaging.

- *Spamming attacks*: Electronic message system is used by the OSN users to send malicious contents like fraudulent advertisement to other users. This message influences the user to create fake profiles in the same or different networks. According to the report, the leading OSNs like Facebook and YouTube broadcast spam contents compared to other OSNs and media.

- *Malwares*: Malware is nothing but a malicious programmable code consists of viruses, Trojan and worms. Most of the OSNs do not have proper security mechanism to prevent information flow as malicious contents among users. To gather the personal information of any account and harm the system, malicious information may be spread by fake or legitimate users on OSN platforms (Al-Qurishi et al., 2018; Li, Deng, Gupta, Wang, & Choi 2019; Zhang, Jing, Wang, Choo, & Gupta, 2020). The first worm named Koobface propagated through Facebook and later spread to other OSNs like Twitter and MySpace. According to a survey, the AV-TEST Institute registers more than 3.9 lakhs new malicious per day. All these contents are detected by various malicious detection tools like Sunshine and V Test which are separated based on their features and saved (Sahoo & Gupta, 2019a).

- *Ransomware*: It is a special kind of malicious code that blocks access to a computer until the asked money is paid to the attackers. According to the Barkly survey report, a corporate faced ransomware attack at every 40 seconds (Yang et al., 2015). The percentage of ransomware attacks in different corporate sectors affected has raised in recent years.

- *OSN aggregator*: It furnishes the facility to combined different information from various online utilities and social networks into a single environment. An attacker can use OSN aggregator to gather appropriate information about the OSN user from various sites.

Later, adversary uses this accumulated information to do various attacks on OSNs (Dürr, Werner, & Maier, 2010).

- *Malicious URLs*: Fake profile users share attractive information using website URLs. Also, OSN users broadcast important information to their friends through these URLs. In OSN, malicious URLs (Su, Wu, Lee, & Wei, 2013) are spread as posts, likes, or comments.
- An adversary shares various malicious links through URL posting feature option. They can reduce these URLs using various methods and facilities such as bit.ly. The short URLs can embed and hide original URLs. Also, the suspicious websites can hide behind these URLs. As a result, it can spread in the form of spamming- and phishing-based threats on various OSNs.
- *Cross-site request forgery*: It is not a kind of threat but it is a mechanism applied to diffuse an advanced OSN worm. After login to users' browser, this threat exploits the trust of OSN users. The attackers can easily post an image in a user's event stream, as long as the social network applications do not check the referrer header (Siddiqui & Verma, 2011).

2.5.3 Social Threats

To stalk and provoke the people in social network platforms, adversary uses social threat. This threat targeted young and teenagers deliberately. Due to the serious concern, certain remedies are required to handle these threats in social network platforms.

- *Online predators*: Through social network platforms, online predator is one who commits child sexual assault. Behaviour which is considered to be in the Internet sexual victimisation is shown to develop teenager pornography (Anand, Kumar, & Anand, 2017). Most of the time, children are unaware of their discussion with other users and the kinship intensifies to a real-life confluence and attracts inappropriate activities.
- *Cyber stalking*: It is a criminal activity in which the attackers harass a social network user by sending emails and instant messaging. Many times, OSN users share their location through posting. An adversary can collect their information using content-based retrieval methods. This leads to the misuse of information and execute hazardous social engineering attack.
- *Corporate espionage*: Corporate espionage always tries to execute automated social engineering attacks using various social network

platforms. An attacker collected personal information such as status and position of the employee, email ID, and cell number about the employee using OSN instead of classic social engineering approach. The information regarding the adversary is hidden to the victim, if the adversary may be in the same corporate group or in a different group. Taking this advantage, they can easily spread malicious content and harm users' credential without their knowledge.

- *Cyberbullying and grooming*: It is one of the planned processes through which attackers irritate and harm Internet users. Cyber grooming is performed by adults where they exploit children sexually by posting videos on OSN platforms. The age group between 10 and 16 is affected by these issues. The person below this age group is targeted easily by the attackers for cyberbullying attack and highly targeted by an online predator. One example is 'Megan Meier case' that led to the suicide of a girl. Due to the above reason, child safety (Qabajeh, Thabtah, & Chiclana, 2018) is necessary when they are using online social networking.

The above-mentioned types of attack are representative of various threats found on the OSN platforms. The author in Gao, Hu, Huang, Wang, and Yan (2011) analyses different types of attacks on OSNs based on some specific effective parameters which are illustrated in Table 2.1.

TABLE 2.1 Comparison of most popular attacks in OSNs.

DIFFERENT MEASURE	LEAKAGE OF INFORMATION	DE-ANONYMISATION	PHISHING	SYBIL/ FAKE NODES	MALWARE	SPAM-MING
Attack difficulty	Easy to medium	Medium	Easy	Hard	Hard	Easy
Server defence effectiveness	Yes, but with limited effectiveness	No	No	Yes	Yes, but with confined effectiveness	Yes
User defence effectiveness	Yes	No	Yes	No	Yes, but with confined effectiveness	No
Threat to user	High	Medium to high	High	Medium	High	Low

2.6 TAXONOMY OF VARIOUS SOLUTIONS AGAINST OSN ATTACKS

In this section, we discuss an overview of different defensive solution for OSN security and safety. The details of various security solutions based on its categories depicted in Figure 2.2.

2.6.1 In-Built Security Solution

The OSN service providers provide the security-based solutions to its user. Some part of the security solutions is provided at the time of profile creation, and other solutions are provided directly to the users, i.e., the authoritative power of individual account holders to set their privacy settings in their profiles. The social networking operators provide security services like OTP (one-time password) and CAPTCHA (Alsaleh, Alarifi, Al-Salman, Alfayez, & Almuhaysin, 2014), photo identification and multistage authentication principle at the time of creation of profile or at the time of log-in. Every Twitter account goes through two-step authentication security for registration, i.e., in the first step, the user enters his/her user id with password and after that a verification code can generate and redirect that code to the user's mobile phones and registered email. Using this security, authentication can be verified by the Twitter account. Many of the social networking services provide user authentication setting for protecting their account and valuable information from online predators and attackers.

The security setting, at user level, provides the facility to protect the profile according to the user's choice. One of the social networking sites called Facebook provides the security setting like who can visit and see your account like friends, family member, mutual friends, or all. Similarly, Google+ provides grouping facility in a particular account, i.e., users place every account into different groups according to their choice. Some of the service providers provide certain third-party services for security setting by downloading some software. Facebook provides one security system called Facebook immune system to better protect user's accounts from different malwares online.

2.6.2 Third-Party Software Solutions

To protect the OSN users from different threats, some companies offer software-based protection system to operate the profiles in better way. Different

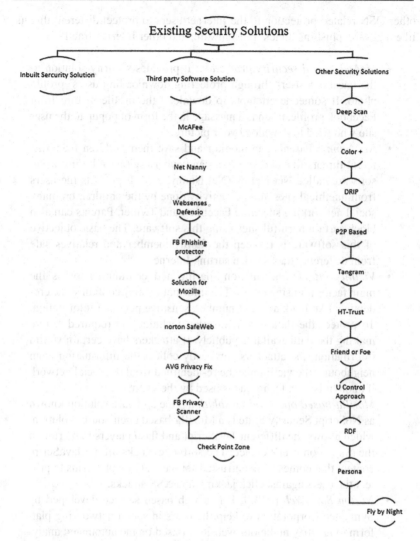

FIGURE 2.2   Existing security solutions for different attacks in online social networks (OSNs).

companies provide different solutions against the cyberattacks such as Kaspersky which protects against malware, anti-theft, and botnet attacks on many social networking platforms. Semantic web-based solution, AVG, Panda, and Ariva offer different types of protection to Internet users, especially OSN users. They provide some software-based firewalls, antivirus, and other OSN-related protection to the Internet users to protect different threats like malware, phishing attack, ransomware, and other Internet fraud.

- *McAfee social security protection*: It provides security solution to the Facebook users through protecting downloading users' profile photo. If someone attempts to download the profile picture from Facebook profile, it sends a message in the form of popup to the user site who tried to download your picture.
- *Net Nanny*: Parents can monitor and save their children from different threats like cyberbullying and cyber espionage by installing software called Net Nanny (Net Nanny, n.d.). It protects the users from unethical sites and the activity done by the children on many social networking sites like Facebook and Twitter. Parents can also block certain harmful sites using this software. The basic objective of this software is to keep the family member and relatives safe from different attacks when surfing Internet.
- *Vicinity attack*: Information sharing and communication is the main factor for using OSNs. The information may contain some credentials like bank account number, sensitive personal information. To protect the data, anonymisation technique is required before making the data available publicly. If attackers have certain victim information, the attackers can easily collect the information from neighbours, the victim may be re-identified from the social network if anonymisation technique is used by the victim.
- *Mozilla-based open-source solution*: One software solution known as NoScript Security Suite is a Mozilla-based open-source solution, which allows the different JavaScript and flash players to be run on the system on user's choice. The software blocks all the JavaScript content that comes from entrusted source on OSN platforms to protect the users against click jacking and XSS attacks.
- *Norton Safe Web (NSW)*: It is a web-based service developed by Symantec Corporation to help the users in social networking platform to identify malicious websites. Based on the automated analysis and feedback of the user, it protects the users from malicious websites. The NSW is a Facebook application with many numbers of users to safeguard the user's privacy.
- *AVG Privacy Fix*: AVG provides web-based security solution on mobile platform called AVG Privacy Fix to protect the OSN users from different attacks. The security solution is a web browser add-on which allows users to manage their account by configuring their privacy setting. The add-on is incorporated into different social network platforms like Facebook, LinkedIn, and Google+ to provide

security to its users. It also tracks the movement of different malicious content and generates a report based on their revenue.

* *Facebook privacy scanner*: Privacy scanner called trend micro is an android-based application used on Facebook platform to protect the system from unauthorised access of data. The application scans the privacy setting of the user, and if some privacy-related concern is in the profile, it informs the user.

* *Checkpoint zone alarm privacy scanner*: It is a Facebook application that monitors the performance of the system by analysing different posts. The security scanner scans the recent activity of the user and generates a report based on its activity. The checkpoint scanner checks all the recent posts or activities in the profile and identifies the posts that disclose the privacy of the users.

2.6.3 Other Security Solutions Against OSN Attacks

In this section, we discuss an overview of different defensive solutions that are developed by different researchers for providing security to OSN users.

* *DeepScan*: *It* is a fake account detection approach proposed by the author in Gong et al. (2018) by analysing users' location-based content using long short-term memory on neural network platform. Certain profile-based features are extracted from various users' account. Later, the authors used various supervised machine learning algorithm to detect fake accounts.

* *Detection of money laundering accounts*: It is intended by the author in Gong et al. (2018) implemented in QQ OSN environment by analysing various profiles features related of different users. They use various profile content features like account viability, transaction details, and spatial correlation between different accounts. This behavioural analysis leads to high true-positive rate with low false-positive rate.

* *Crowd retweeting-based spammer detection*: It is a spammer detection approach proposed by Liu et al. (2018) for analysing spammer tweets in Sina Weibo social network platforms. The tweets are analysed through its content-based features, profile features, social interaction, and the retweet content shared by users. Based on the information gathered from different accounts, the authors use link-based ranking algorithm to identify malicious account.

- *COLOR+*: It is a spammer account detection method in mobile social network using fog computing proposed by the author in Zhang, Li, Wang, Feng, and Guo (2018). This method is lightweight and a fast response method for mobile devices as compared to other methods to detect spammers. It uses interaction content shared over social platforms by various users. The method takes less response time in machine learning and more time to analyse in graph-based approach. This approach can only fit mobile devices.

- *DRIP*: It is used for the detection of malicious account based on the dynamic reputation information propagation proposed by the author in Kefi and Perez (2018). To achieve better detection, rate the author uses request generate by the use for analysis. Each user carries some personal information and sends to various friends who are in contact. At receiver site, the user calculates its comprehensive reputation by combining both direct and indirect contents from sender and their contacts to detect malicious accounts.

- *Detection of human bot, legitimate bot and malicious bot in OSNs based on wavelet*: The author proposed a bot detection method in Aslan, Sağlam, and Li (2018). This method uses an algorithm based on discrete wavelength transformation to obtain a pattern of the information shared by various users as posts. Then, the content is classified using various machine learning algorithms to detect bot account.

- *P2P-based key agreement and batch authentication approach*: It is proposed by the author in Amir, Srinivasan, and Khan (2018) for improving effectiveness and security of peer-to-peer-based OSNs using multiple user authentications simultaneously. The authors demonstrate that the protocols are protected against passive adversaries and impersonator attacks. After examining communicational and computational cost, it supports implicit key validation principle. The principle also supported mutual certification, login to a reputation, community authenticity; non-repudiation, flexibility and access control mechanism.

- *Privacy-preserving friend recommendation scheme*: It is an approached by the author in Guo, Zhang, and Fang (2015). The authors provide various user protection schemes in OSN environment, which includes identity theft, inference attack on online social relationship and fake profile attacks. The proposed method uses friend recommendation system to develop trust relationship and social interaction. It uses multi-hop trust chain for establishing communication in place of single-hop trust relationship. Moreover, this technique creates a privacy-preserving recommendation mechanism for social networks to establish a trust relationship between users.

- *Temple-based spam detector in OSN (Tangram)*: It is proposed by the author in Zhu et al. (2016), for the detection of spammer by filtering non-spammer content in OSNs. It analyses all the generated contents through machine learning platform. For detecting spammer, tangram takes out the template of spammer and compares it with all the generated contents towards precise and quick spam filtering excluding various training phases.
- *A secure and personal auction approach for DOSN*: It is designed by the author in Thapa, Liao, Li, Li, and Sun (2016). This approach helps the user to find malicious accounts by examining intermediate computation in the protocol. This approach protects private as well as user-generated personal information, privacy in e-commerce environment, authenticity and non-repudiation.
- *Secure information hiding via short text*: It is developed by the author in Ren, Liu, and Zhao (2012). This scheme used for hiding personal and profile information in OSNs using text steganography. This scheme protects user content information when users share and posts information publicly on the social network platforms. By this process, the shared content information can be protected against unauthorised person who tries to access and gather users' personal information.
- *MPAC (multiparty access control)*: It is an approach proposed by the author in Hu, Ahn, and Jorgensen (2013). This approach hides personal identity that is shared among various users on different social networks such as date of birth, phone number, gender, personal address, and bank details publicly. By this process, it protects the user information by capturing authorisation principle. Also this approach applies collaborative management of shared data along with a multiparty policy specification scheme and corresponding policy evaluation mechanism (Bahwaireth, Tawalbeh, Benkhelifa, Jararweh, & Tawalbeh, 2016).
- *Hybrid trust evaluation approach (HT–TRUST)*: This approach proposed by the author in Zhang, Yong, Li, Pan, and Huang (2017). This approach used factor enhancement-based hybrid trust approach for trust measurement in e-commerce social networks. Sometimes it is hard to identify trusted user in spite of users' good reputation and high-profile rating. This approach furnishes an authentic and secure social platform for e-commerce management to generate trust between the users in OSNs platform.
- *Secure data sharing scheme (CP-ABPRE)*: It is proposed by the author in Qinlong, Zhaofeng Yixian, Xinxin, and Jingyi (2014). This is used to protect OSN users' information and private information.

By accessing the customised access policy data, it outsources coded data to various OSNs. By using symmetric key encryption algorithm, the authors encoded the data with the help of random key. Then the authors applied different access policy principles.

- *Friend or foes*: The authors proposed one distributed randomised algorithm in Li and Lui (2014). For finding a dishonest recommendation on OSN, the authors provide various algorithms. This proposed randomised algorithm identifies such dishonest friend requests from various users on the same or different networks to protect sensitive and valuable information. To identify various dishonest accounts, the proposed algorithm implemented in various social network platforms.
- *The U-control approach*: This approach presented by the author in Shin, Lopes, Claycomb, and Ahn (2009). It allows social network users to deal with the allocation of their personal information and to maintain a level of their secrecy on social network platforms. It provides digital persona and privacy management. By this approach, legitimate users cannot assure their privacy. Furthermore, this approach is based on OSN service provider's existence. Using various encryption techniques, it hides the user's personal information and communication against another party on OSN.
- *The flyByNight architecture*: It is proposed by the author in Lucas and Borisov (2008). It is designed to care for the privacy of users' personal information shared among registered Facebook users. In this, OSN users encrypt their confidential information using client-side JavaScript. So, confidential information cannot be ascertained by the OSN servers. For encoding the content, public-key encryption algorithm is used. Furthermore, the operator provides various protection mechanisms because the entire cryptographic algorithm is done inside users' home page with client-side JavaScript code. For management of key attributes, the flyByNight Architecture used at server ends. It is flexible to normal user and OSN dependent (can be used only for Facebook).
- *FaceCloak architecture* (Luo, Xie, & Hengartner, 2009): By this architecture, it is planned to hide private information of OSN users without using any additional configuration or installation of software by the user. It provides security to social network users by protecting confidential data. It also encrypting these data with the help of symmetric key encryption. By this architecture, confidential data are replaced by fake ones, while the encrypted content is maintained on a third-party server. The user, who has the required the key, can decipher the ciphered data stored on the third-party

server. This architecture depends on existing social network service provider for implementation.

- *Secret Interest Groups* (SIGs): This approach proposed by the author in Sorniotti and Molva (2010) to extenuate the users' communication privacy in various OSNs. However, for the protection of users' public information, it does not provide a direct solution, but it gives a platform for attaining self-managed groups (about private, sensitive, or secret topics) and for managing the members of these groups. Moreover, by using this approach, each user is totally free to decide who can access their private information. It does not demand a centralised feature but it functions in a circulated fashion.

- *Virtual private social network (VPSN)* (Conti, Hasani, & Crispo, 2011): It is used for the protection of user content in OSNs. VSPN is completely based on the concept of virtual private network. It uses existing social network infrastructure and their users. It operates through creating a private link in between VPSN members to share secret information. Other users of the underlying OSN and the OSN administrator also are not able to access the same information. It can be viewed as an artillery to defeat users' privacy threats in various OSNs and a privacy-conscious OSNs without the prerequisite of handling OSN infrastructure.

- *Decision recommendation system for sharing image* (Hu, Chen, Wu, & Zhao, 2017): It is an approach for calculating the privacy level of a digital image in the profile, based on perceptual hashing and semantic privacy rules. Some of the threats download the profile photo of the user and use the same to create different accounts in the same platform or different platforms. By this way, the people can gather personal information of the users, including the profile pictures to spread malicious content on the web.

- *ReDS (a back-propagation technique)*: It is an approach used to enhance the safety of data in P2P-based network. This approach does not need much user participation for operation. It operates directly on the network based on the principles and features. Using authentication and encryption mechanism, it protects the personal information of the user and confidential data also. This technique does not provide the backup facility to the user and also to the users' accounts (Keretna, Hossny, & Creighton, 2013).

- *RDF (resource description approach)*: The RDF approach does not require much participation from the user, it executes at the server end and operates at operator site. The service provider uses this approach to separate the data into different subsets and implements certain encryption techniques to protect the user data and confidential information. The approach uses the principle of encryption and decryption technique to protect the user data from unauthorised access (Carminati, Ferrari, Heatherly, Kantarcioglu, & Thurainsingham, 2009).

- *Mechanism based on re-socialising*: This technique is based on the principle of coupling and out-of-bound invitation for designing multi-domain OSNs. The concept of re-socialising in OSN platforms is for communication purposes between different users in the same network. The service providers provide the authentication principles for better protection of the user content at their end. The different encryption techniques and methods are also implemented by the service provider to protect the valuable information.

- *Virtual personal server*: It (Cáceres, Cox, Lim, Shakimov, & Varshavsky, 2009) is a virtual machine installed at the user computer to protect the data against the different attacks. The virtual machine installed at the user site creates a copy of the entire OSN sites. The user can install the third-party applications and services also using this virtual machine. After creating the copy of the OSN, it can operate the account by any means without getting affected by the attackers. To better protect accounts, the user itself can manage the platform and set up their configuration for suitable operations.

- *Persona* (Starin, Baden, Bender, Spring, & Bhattacharjee, 2009): To provide data access control policy on OSN platform, researchers have designed an effective way of generating application for the OSN users. To protect the personal data of the user, it uses access control policy called attribute-based encryption techniques. The approach works like an API in Facebook platform to protect the user from unauthorised access. The API is implemented with the help of Firefox extension for compilation of markup languages. The approach or API can be easily installed in the computer of Facebook users and also uninstalled easily.

- *Machine learning–based fake account detector* (Xiao, Freeman, & Hwa, 2015): In this approach, it uses some machine learning pipeline approach for detecting fake accounts on OSN like Facebook, LinkedIn, etc. The actor-based classification of accounts is grouped into different clusters so that the identification of the fake account can be easier by analysing clusters. The basic objective of the approach is to identify the actor of the individual cluster to know if the account is from the same actor or from different.

- *Facebook Inspector (FBI)*: This approach is used to provide the real-time solution for identifying malicious content on Facebook platform. The approach analyses the different characteristics of the Facebook profile and categorised the content into two different groups based on their behaviour and activities. It processes a pre-trained approach on different characteristics to know the exact behaviour of the system. It detects the malicious content available on the user profile by analysing post, blog, message, and chat rooms.

- *Audit and analysis of imposters*: It is an experimental approach for detecting fake accounts in OSN. The approach is implemented on the individual profiles by analysing the friends and mutual friends of the account holder. The approach is only applicable to the Facebook profiles. The approach classifies the profile information on the basis of public data available and process through machine learning algorithm with different classification techniques.

- *COMPA: A behavioural feature-based analysis* (Egele, Stringhini, Kruegel, & Vigna, 2013): COMPA is a tool-based detection technique of fake profiles on different OSN platforms. It can be installed at the users' computer, and when the user uses the social networking sites, it is automatically incorporated with the user profile and analyses the features associated with the account.

- *Fake Spotter*: It (Freeman, 2017) is an approach for finding fake accounts in OSN platforms by sending certain feedback-related question to different users who are in their friend list. All the feedbacks are collected and stored in the database and certain analysis principles on those feedbacks are used to get the information about the user. The approach set an index level based on the feedback question. When all the feedbacks pass that approach, it creates a similarity index for finding legitimate or fake profile activities. The approach is only implemented on the LinkedIn platform.

- *Friend in the middle (FIM)* (Beato et al., 2013): It is a technique to resilient de-anonymisation technique on OSN platform. It provides a gateway to connect two different accounts in the same platform to avoid the attacks from different profiles. The approach creates a path between two users after verifying the content of the users and the activities done by the users on its profile.

- *FRAppE-based malicious App detector* (Gurumurthy, Sushama, Ramu, & Nikhitha, 2019): For detecting malicious content on the Facebook platform, Rahman et al. proposed a solution called FRAppE tool, which is focused on detecting malicious application and in-built with Facebook profiles. The observation of the account can be done by collecting the information from different accounts. The different apps that are found in different profiles are combined in a particular location and based on certain parameters like activity, user interaction; however, the applications are segregated into two different categories called benign and fake applications.

- *Actor approach-based fraud detector*: Kelvin et al. proposed an approach for detecting fraud on OSNs based on graph-based approach. The approach analyses the different actor and their characteristics in the network platform for detecting fraudulent content. The approach identifies the number of links available in the profile and then analyses the content by the help of machine learning principles to detect malicious content attached to that link.

2.7 CHAPTER SUMMARY

OSNs provide different facilities and services for information sharing and communication to automate our day-to-day task. It also aids by furnishing security solutions. People spend their valuable time surfing the Internet and use OSNs to do their work in their day-to-day life. OSN users enjoy when they use OSN to communicate with others and share their experience and knowledge, pictures, videos, texts, and much more without geographical and economical limitations. By considering the social platform as a preferred way of communication, this chapter highlights various issues and threats associated with every account with various defensive approaches for solving those issues. Particularly, it climaxes various opportunities that help their users for bringing them in front.

REFERENCES

Al-Qurishi, M., Rahman, S. M. M., Alamri, A., Mostafa, M. A., Al-Rubaian, M., Hossain, M. S., & Gupta, B. B. (2018). SybilTrap: A graph-based semi-supervised Sybil defense scheme for online social networks. *Concurrency and Computation: Practice and Experience*, 30(5), e4276.

Alsaleh, M., Alarifi, A., Al-Salman, A. M., Alfayez, M., & Almuhaysin, A. (2014). TSD: Detecting Sybil accounts in twitter. *Proceedings – 2014 13th international conference on machine learning and applications, ICMLA 2014*, 463–469. https://doi.org/10.1109/ICMLA.2014.81.

Al-Zoubi, A. M., Alqatawna, J., & Faris, H. (2017). Spam profile detection in social networks based on public features. *2017 8th international conference on information and communication systems, ICICS 2017*. https://doi.org/10.1109/IACS.2017.7921959.

Amir, A., Srinivasan, B., & Khan, A. I. (2018). Distributed classification for image spam detection. *Multimedia Tools and Applications, 77*(11), 13249–13278.

Anand, K., Kumar, J., & Anand, K. (2017). Anomaly detection in online social network: A survey. *Proceedings of the International Conference on Inventive Communication and Computational Technologies, 39*, 456–459. doi: https://doi.org/10.1109/ICICCT.2017.7975239. ICICCT 2017.

Aslan, Ç. B., Sağlam, R. B., & Li, S. (2018). Automatic detection of cyber security related accounts on online social networks: Twitter as an example. *ACM international conference proceeding series*, 236–240. https://doi.org/10.1145/3217804.3217919.

Bahwaireth, K., Tawalbeh, L., Benkhelifa, E., Jararweh, Y., & Tawalbeh, M. A. (2016). Experimental comparison of simulation tools for efficient cloud and mobile cloud computing applications. *Eurasip Journal on Information Security*, (1). doi: https://doi.org/10.1186/s13635-016-0039-y.

Beato, F., Conti, M., & Preneel, B. (2013). Friend in the Middle (FiM): Tackling deanonymization in social networks. *2013 IEEE international conference on pervasive computing and communications workshops, PerCom workshops 2013, March*, 279–284. https://doi.org/10.1109/PerComW.2013.6529495.

Cáceres, R., Cox, L., Lim, H., Shakimov, A., & Varshavsky, A. (2009). Virtual individual servers as privacy-preserving proxies for mobile devices,. In *1st ACM Workshop on Networking, Systems, and Applications for Mobile Handhelds, ACM* (pp. 37–42).

Campos, S. B. Jr., Tavares, G. F., Igawa, G. M., & Guido, M. L. P. Jr., R. C. (2018). Detection of human, legitimate bot, and malicious bot in online social networks based on wavelets. *ACM Transactions on Multimedia Computing, Communications, and Applications, 14*(1s), 1–17. doi: https://doi.org/10.1145/3183506.

Carminati, B., Ferrari, E., Heatherly, R., Kantarcioglu, M., & Thurainsingham, B. (2009). A semantic web based framework for social network access control. *Proceedings of ACM symposium on access control models and technologies, SACMAT, January*, 177–186. https://doi.org/10.1145/1542207.1542237.

Conti, M., Hasani, A., & Crispo, B. (2011). *Virtual private social networks. January*, 39–50. doi: https://doi.org/10.1145/1943513.1943521.

Dewan, P. (2017). Facebook inspector (FbI): Towards automatic real-time detection of malicious content on Facebook. *Social Network Analysis and Mining, 7*(1), 1–25. doi: https://doi.org/10.1007/s13278-017-0434-5.

Ding, X., Zhang, L., Wan, Z., & Gu, M. (2010). A brief survey on de-anonymization attacks in online social networks. *Proceedings – International conference on computational aspects of social networks, CASoN'10*, 611–615. https://doi.org/10.1109/CASoN.2010.139.

Dürr, M., Werner, M., & Maier, M. (2010). Re-socializing online social networks. *Proceedings – 2010 IEEE/ACM international conference on green computing and communications, GreenCom 2010, 2010 IEEE/ACM international conference on cyber, physical and social computing, CPSCom 2010, January 2011*, 786–791. https://doi.org/10.1109/GreenCom-CPSCom.2010.18.

Egele, M., Stringhini, G., Kruegel, C., & Vigna., G. (2013). COMPA: Detecting compromised accounts on social networks. *ISOC network and distributed systems symposium (NDSS)*.

Freeman, D. M. (2017). Can you spot the fakes? On the limitations of user feedback in online social networks. *26th international world wide web conference, WWW 2017*, 1093–1102. https://doi.org/10.1145/3038912.3052706.

Gao, H., Hu, J., Huang, T., & Wang, J., and Yan C. (2011). Security issues in online social networks. *IEEE Internet Computing, 15*(4), 56–63. doi: https://doi.org/ doi:10.1109/MIC.2011.50.

Gong, Q., Chen, Y., He, X., Zhuang, Z., Wang, T., Huang, H., ... Fu, X. (2018). DeepScan: Exploiting deep learning for malicious account detection in location-based social networks. *IEEE Communications Magazine, 56*(11), 21–27. doi: https://doi.org/10.1109/MCOM.2018.1700575.

Guo, L., Zhang, C., & Fang, Y. (2015). A trust-based privacy-preserving friend recommendation Scheme for online social networks. *IEEE Transactions on Dependable and Secure Computing, 12*(4), 413–427. doi: https://doi.org/10.1109/ TDSC.2014.2355824.

Gupta, S., & Gugulothu, N. (2018). Secure NoSQL for the social networking and e-commerce based bigdata applications deployed in cloud. *International Journal of Cloud Applications and Computing (IJCAC), 8*(2), 113–129.

Gupta, S., Gupta, B. B., & Chaudhary, P. (2019). A client-server JavaScript code rewriting-based framework to detect the XSS worms from online social network. *Concurrency and Computation: Practice and Experience, 31*(21), e4646.

Gurumurthy, S., Sushama, C., Ramu, M., & Nikhitha, K. S. (2019). Design and implementation of intelligent system to detect malicious Facebook posts using support vector machine (SVM). *SpringerBriefs in applied sciences and technology* (pp. 17–24). https://doi.org/10.1007/978-981-13-0059-2_3.

Hu, H., Ahn, G. J., & Jorgensen, J. (2013). Multiparty access control for online social networks: Model and mechanisms. *IEEE Transactions on Knowledge and Data Engineering, 25*(7), 1614–1627. doi: https://doi.org/10.1109/TKDE.2012.97.

Hu, D., Chen, F., Wu, X., & Zhao, Z. (2017). A framework of privacy decision recommendation for image sharing in online social networks. *Proceedings – 2016 IEEE 1st international conference on data science in cyberspace, DSC 2016, June 2016*, 243–251. https://doi.org/10.1109/DSC.2016.100.

Jorquera Valero, J. M., Sánchez Sánchez, P. M., Fernández Maimó, L., Huertas Celdrán, A., Arjona Fernández, M., De Los Santos Vílchez, S., & Martínez Pérez, G. (2018). Improving the security and QoE in mobile devices through an intelligent and adaptive continuous authentication system. *Sensors (Basel, Switzerland), 18*(11), 1–29. doi: https://doi.org/10.3390/s18113769.

Kefi, H., & Perez, C. (2018). Dark Side of online social networks: Technical, managerial, and behavioral perspectives. *Encyclopedia of social network analysis and mining* (pp. 1–22). https://doi.org/10.1007/978-1-4614-7163-9_110217-1.

Keretna, S., Hossny, A., & Creighton, D. (2013). Recognising user identity in twitter social networks via text mining. *Proceedings – 2013 IEEE international conference on systems, man, and cybernetics, SMC 2013*, 3079–3082. https://doi. org/10.1109/SMC.2013.525.

Koll, D., Schwarzmaier, M., Li, J., Li, X. Y., & Fu, X. (2017). Thank you for being a friend: An attacker view on online-social-network-based Sybil defenses. *Proceedings – IEEE 37th international conference on distributed computing systems workshops, ICDCSW 2017, i*, 157–162. https://doi.org/10.1109/ ICDCSW.2017.67.

Li, D., Deng, L., Gupta, B. B., Wang, H., & Choi, C. (2019). A novel CNN based security guaranteed image watermarking generation scenario for smart city applications. *Information Sciences, 479,* 432–447.

Li, Y., & Lui, J. C. S. (2014). Friends or foes: Distributed and randomized algorithms to determine dishonest recommenders in online social networks. *IEEE Transactions on Information Forensics and Security, 9*(10), 1695–1707. doi: https://doi.org/10.1109/TIFS.2014.2346020.

Liu, B., Ni, Z., Luo, J., Cao, J., Ni, X., Liu, B., & Fu, X. (2018). Analysis of and defense against crowd-retweeting based spam in social networks. *World Wide Web, 22*(6), 2953–2975.

Lucas, M. M., & Borisov, N. (2008). FlyByNight: Mitigating the privacy risks of social networking. *Proceedings of the 7th ACM workshop on privacy in the electronic society – WPES '08,* 1. https://doi.org/10.1145/1456403.1456405.

Luo, W., Xie, Q., & Hengartner, U. (2009). FaceCloak: An architecture for user privacy on social networking sites. *Proceedings – 12th IEEE international conference on computational science and engineering, CSE 2009, 3,* 26–33. doi: https://doi.org/10.1109/CSE.2009.387.

Mislove, A., Viswanath, B., Gummadi, K. P., & Druschel, P. (2010). You are who you know: Inferring user profiles in online social networks. *Wsdm,* 251–260. https://doi.org/10.1145/1718487.1718519.

Narain, Y., Kumar, S., & Gupta, P. (2012). Fusion of electrocardiogram with unobtrusive biometrics : An efficient individual authentication system. *Pattern Recognition Letters, 33*(14), 1932–1941. doi: https://doi.org/10.1016/j.patrec.2012.03.010.

Net Nanny. (n.d.). www.netnanny.com. Accessed on July 2020.

(2011). Usability and security aspects social network sites (sns). *ICTACT Journal on Communication Technology, 02*(04), 463–467. doi: https://doi.org/10.21917/ijct.2011.0065.

Palmieri, F., Fiore, U., & Castiglione, A. (2011). Automatic security assessment for next generation wireless mobile networks. *Mobile Information Systems, 7*(3), 217–239. doi: https://doi.org/10.3233/MIS-2011-0119.

Qabajeh, I., Thabtah, F., & Chiclana, F. (2018). A recent review of conventional vs. automated cybersecurity anti-phishing techniques. *Computer Science Review, 29,* 44–55. doi: https://doi.org/10.1016/j.cosrev.2018.05.003.

Qinlong, H., Zhaofeng, M., Yixian, Y., Xinxin, N., & Jingyi, F. (2014). Improving security and efficiency for encrypted data sharing in online social networks. *China Communications, 11*(3), 104–117. doi: https://doi.org/10.1109/cc.2014.6825263.

Ren, W., Liu, Y., & Zhao, J. (2012). Provably secure information hiding via short text in social networking tools. *Tsinghua Science and Technology, 17*(3), 225–231. doi: https://doi.org/10.1109/TST.2012.6216751.

Sadhya, D., & Singh, S. K. (2017). Providing robust security measures to bloom filter based biometric template protection schemes. *Computers and Security, 67,* 59–72. doi: https://doi.org/10.1016/j.cose.2017.02.013.

Sahoo, S. R., & Gupta, B. B. (2019a). Classification of various attacks and their defence mechanism in online social networks : A survey. *Enterprise Information Systems,* 1–33. doi: https://doi.org/10.1080/17517575.2019.1605542.

Sahoo, S. R., & Gupta, B. B. (2019b). Hybrid approach for detection of malicious profiles in twitter. *Computers and Electrical Engineering, 76,* 65–81. doi: https://doi.org/10.1016/j.compeleceng.2019.03.003.

Sahoo, S. R., & Gupta, B. B. (2020). Fake profile detection in multimedia big data on online social networks. *International Journal of Information and Computer Security, 12*(2–3), 303–331.

Sarode, A. J., & Mishra, A. (2015). Audit and analysis of impostors: An experimental approach to detect fake profile in online social network. *ACM international conference proceeding series, 25–27-Sept,* 1–8. https://doi.org/10.1145/2818567.2818568.

Shin, D., Lopes, R., Claycomb, W., & Ahn, G. J. (2009). A framework for enabling user-controlled persona in online social networks. *Proceedings – International Computer Software and Applications Conference, 1,* 292–297. doi: https://doi.org/10.1109/COMPSAC.2009.46.

Siddiqui, H., Brill, C., Davis, Z., & Olmsted, A. (2016). Friend or Faux? Engineering your social network to detect fraudulent profiles. *In Information Society (i-Society), 2016 international conference,* 169–170.

Siddiqui, M. S., & Verma, D. (2011). Cross site request forgery: A common web application weakness. *2011 IEEE 3rd international conference on communication software and networks, ICCSN 2011,* 538–543. https://doi.org/10.1109/ICCSN.2011.6014783.

Sorniotti, A., & Molva, R. (2010, March). Secret interest groups (SIGs) in social networks with an implementation on Facebook. In Proceedings of the 2010 ACM Symposium on Applied Computing (pp. 621–628). doi: https://doi.org/10.1145/1774088.1774219.

Starin, D., Baden, R., Bender, A., Spring, N., & Bhattacharjee, B. (2009). Persona : An online social network with user-defined privacy categories and subject descriptors. *Sigcomm, 09,* 135–146. doi: https://doi.org/10.1145/1592568.1592585.

Su, K. W., Wu, K. P., Lee, H. M., & Wei, T. E. (2013). Suspicious URL filtering based on logistic regression with multi-view analysis. *Proceedings – 2013 8th Asia joint conference on information security, Asia JCIS 2013,* 77–84. https://doi.org/10.1109/ASIAJCIS.2013.19.

Thapa, A., Liao, W., Li, M., Li, P., & Sun, J. (2016). SPA: A secure and private auction framework for decentralized online social networks. *IEEE Transactions on Parallel and Distributed Systems, 27*(8), 2394–2407. doi: https://doi.org/10.1109/TPDS.2015.2494009.

Tian, Y., Yuan, J., & Yu, S. (2017). SBPA: Social behavior based cross social network phishing attacks. *2016 IEEE conference on communications and network security, CNS 2016,* 366–367. https://doi.org/10.1109/CNS.2016.7860514.

Xiao, C., Freeman, D. M., & Hwa, T. (2015). *Detecting clusters of fake accounts in online social networks.* https://doi.org/10.1145/2808769.2808779.

Yang, T., Yang, Y., Qian, K., Lo, D. C. T., Qian, Y., & Tao, L. (2015). Automated detection and analysis for android ransomware. *Proceedings – 2015 IEEE 17th international conference on high performance computing and communications, 2015 IEEE 7th international symposium on cyberspace safety and security and 2015 IEEE 12th international conference on embedded software and systems, H, 1,* 1338–1343. https://doi.org/10.1109/HPCC-CSS-ICESS.2015.39.

Zhang, X. L., He, X. Y., Yu, F. M., Liu, L. X., Zhang, H. X., & Li, Z. L. (2019). Distributed and personalised social network privacy protection. *International Journal of High Performance Computing and Networking, 13*(2), 153–163.

Zhang, Z., Jing, J., Wang, X., Choo, K. K. R., & Gupta, B. B. (2020). A crowdsourcing method for online social networks security assessment based on human-centric computing. *Human-centric Computing and Information Sciences*, *10*(1), 1–19.

Zhang, J., Li, Q., Wang, X., Feng, B., & Guo, D. (2018). Towards fast and lightweight spam account detection in mobile social networks through fog computing. *Peer-to-Peer Networking and Applications*, *11*(4), 778–792. doi: https://doi.org/10.1007/s12083-017-0559-3.

Zhang, B., Yong, R., Li, M., Pan, J., & Huang, J. (2017). A hybrid trust evaluation framework for E-commerce in online social network: A factor enrichment perspective. *IEEE Access*, *5*, 7080–7096. doi: https://doi.org/10.1109/ACCESS.2017.2692249.

Zhang, X., Zheng, H., Li, X., Du, S., & Zhu, H. (2014). You are where you have been: Sybil detection via geo-location analysis in OSNs. *2014 IEEE Global communications conference, GLOBECOM 2014*, 698–703. https://doi.org/10.1109/GLOCOM.2014.7036889.

Zheng, H., He, J., Zhang, Y., Wu, J., & Ji, Z. (2019). A mathematical model for intimacy-based security protection in social network without violation of privacy. *International Journal of High Performance Computing and Networking*, *15*(3–4), 121–132.

Zhu, T., Gao, H., Yang, Y., Bu, K., Chen, Y., Downey, D., … Choudhary, A. N. (2016). Beating the artificial chaos: Fighting OSN spam using its own templates. *IEEE/ACM Transactions on Networking*, *24*(6), 3856–3869. doi: https://doi.org/10.1109/TNET.2016.2557849.

Fundamentals of Online Social Networks (OSNs) and Opportunities

3

This chapter describes various opportunities provided to social network users and branding their products through advertisements. It also describes the opportunities and methods provided to the users for interaction with customers and building social relationships. Furthermore, this chapter elaborates on how the information flows between different users and engages social network users. Finally, this chapter provides a deep incites related to various opportunities and their consequences, including the social threats that hamper user credentials.

3.1 OPPORTUNITIES IN SOCIAL MEDIA

Online social network (OSN) or media bid individuals and business personnel a lot of opportunities that did not available previously. It provides a new way to connect people all over of the world in an interesting way and also ability to manage their content what people can see. People also configure their account based on their usage and other users' choice. It is an efficient and simple way where a normal post from the user can be read by many people in the same or different community. Through this process, a user of OSNs can post advertisements and get RSVPs without direct communication with publics (Gupta, Gupta, & Chaudhary, 2018). Through this virtual way of communication, various users achieve their goals without any substantial technical aids.

The benefit of using social network platform may be of greater importance in some way but in some instances, it helps the personal life of the people a bit. Also, for business OSNs offer different organisations the way to reach various customers in a new way. To promote the product as well as raise the corporate awareness, different organisation fix a target people to purchase their products (Sahoo & Gupta, 2019a). It also a platform to engage consumers, provide a platform for commination and interaction with them, and increase customer in your area or even where the product is available. The platform provides an interface for social network account users and allows the users to operate the profile easily like Facebook and Twitter on a mobile which are the common application in these fields (Gupta et al., 2018; Stergiou, Psannis, Xifilidis, Plageras, & Gupta, 2018; Al-Qurishi et al., 2018).

One of the famous and popular sites called foursquare.com provides various location awareness with complete details about various stores, restaurants, and other venues close to users' area (Kefi & Perez, 2018). The user also follows various comments posted by different users and the check-in features to show that you visited. Through these sites, people also get information regarding various discounts and offers related to products. Furthermore, OSNs provide various opportunities for marketing different products such as new and existing and advertise different brands (Alghamdi, Watson, & Xu, 2017).

3.2 BRANDING

A brand is nothing but one identifiable image that belongs to a particular individual or business. People associated with this can identify the market. In regard to marketing, it is just an identification in terms of logo, slogan, name of company or individuals, or an idea familiar to consumers (Tous et al., 2018). As a platform of social media, it provides opportunity for their customers to advertise their product, branding through logo and other publishing contents. Consistency and inconsistency are two different parameters in branding when user posts or shares their content over Internet. When a person creates an account in social network sites, s/he may decide to attach one image in the form of logo by changing profile appearances to match others' account. When any user looks for a specific account in different social platforms like Facebook, Twitter, they are getting confused regarding the official mail (Sahoo & Gupta, 2019b). To avoid such circumstances, companies should develop the design document that outlines the branding the products. At least the product contains the following:

- Information of the brand with its colour specification.
- The font and the style used.

- The way in which the product or business name specified.
- Specific logos with colour combination.
- The style, design, and illustration so that the representation of the content image should be consistent.

3.3 BUILDING OF SOCIAL AUTHORITY IN SOCIAL PLATFORM

The reputation of a profile or a community depends on its behaviour in social platform based on the content posted or shared. That also represents the effectivity of profile, because twitting or posting a content in social platform can result a lot based on responses of different users in their list or other communities. The information shared among users is the major part of social network interaction. So, to build up the reputation in social network through social authority is a major role. The social authority shows the user' and organisation's expertise on their contents (Zhu et al., 2016). The factors that influence the social authority are based on the 3W, i.e. who you know, what they know, and how they know regarding these contents. The simplest way to identify or figure out the social authority is analysing and looking to profile friend and followers. As an example, if I follow more people on Twitter than following, then I said others are influencing towards me. In other way, we can say, if a person has more friends and followers, that person reaches a large audience and influences a lot of people. The social authority is very important due to the image of the company as well as for reputation of the organisation, including better search engine optimisation ranking. For an example, search engine like Google and Bing in social network platform ranked the search result based on their usage (Mateen, Iqbal, Aleem, & Islam et al., 2017). The search engine uses the robotic principle to manage the content like social bookmarking, content generated by the user, links, shares, and various information in the form of posts or tweets in Twitter, Instagram, LinkedIn, Google+, Pinterest, and YouTube. The generated contents are managed through links in Google search for better clarity and understanding. Out of all these contents generated through various users in social platform, links have the higher social authority with greater importance (Carullo et al., 2013). The best practice is to increase the social authority and attract more people towards users' social network account through honestly and genuinely. If the posted information have authentic proof, people will accept that information and the reputation of your account will increase, and the followers too.

3.4 CUSTOMERS' ENGAGEMENT

The people or organisation who use social media forget that it's social. The content shared by them reaches every person who is associated with the same platform directly and indirectly. It is not about only posting information, it is a genuine and reputable environment in the form of virtual information sharing and communication. Also, a social media platform is more suitable for direct marketing and acquiring social reputation and respect based on interest of people (Al-Zoubi, Alqatawna, & Faris, 2017).

When people use a social network as a virtual communication, they must know and feel a part of what they are getting. As an example, if an organisation is involved with any charity work and is associated with that page, people need to know about it. The content shared on the social platform is interesting and entertaining to the viewer as a potential customer (Agrawal, Wang, Sahoo, & Gupta, 2019). In this process, the directing of human imagination and attention towards to a specific content is important.

3.5 SENDING THE WORD OUT

The various opportunities provided by the social network platforms for a specific business can be pretty extensive, but the main benefit is the capability to influence people for different benefits such as, advertising, products, sales, business, events, and specific services offered by you. To reach wide audience, this platform behaves as a tool for transforming content and other things also. Also, that will reach a wide range of people when we use different kinds of social network platforms for application (Sahoo & Gupta, 2020). Although it is not specific for professional contents, you can combine multiple contents like authentic information with user-generated professional graphics and advertisements. Creating user-generated information is somehow pointless because no one will read that. So, information should post in such a way that seems to be genuine and helps the user a lot. To attract people through other users account is also a prominent way for posting advertisement.

The place where the most recommended site for posting advertisement is official website. It is a better practise to add links in Twitter and Facebook to follow you. The customer who viewed your post must access the social media content with their own social network page like Facebook, Twitter, and in other media-related profiles too (Chaudhary & Gupta, 2017). The user also has the provision to share the posted content of other profiles through share option and that can be viewed by other users in the same group as well as in different groups. If the user includes various information like their address, phone number, and other information on their profile page, it is visible to their friends and friends of friends that may create a big trouble at latter, because all this information used by various intruders to conduct some malicious activities.

If the person has a Facebook account, they must have the knowledge regarding the status update page. This feature provides all sort of information regarding to any users (Agrawal et al., 2019). Many users share their content like relationship status, date of birth, birth of their children, project-related contents, and other information too. However, the user must pay attention regarding that content when they share that information.

3.6 WHAT TO SAY? AND WHAT NOT TO?

The information shared by the people in social network platforms through tweets and posts are informal, genuine messages, and also quick. It is always a better practice too thick for a while before commenting. It is also very important to consider what not to mention against those tweets. Replying too much or less are also embarrassing and leads the organisation into taking some legal action (Guo, Zhang, & Fang, 2015). Also, it leads to some security issues related to profile activities and others.

Various organisation follow some strict regulation, legislation, and restriction that restrict to publish some contents. Also, these rules protect user information that become public. Sensitive issues related to medical should be kept private. Because all the issues may mislead others those are in social network platform. Also, some laws are imposed to prevent publishing someone's name if that person is under a particular age. If police, or some authority posted certain information related to any crime and that hamper the users' name and fame, it violates that person's right. To protect yourself and the profile information related to individual or company from some criminal activities, you must ensure that you are following the fixed parameter (Liang, Chen, & Wu, 2018).

When the person shares their account details in the social network platforms, they must know about the security setting who can see those details. For these the user must aware regarding the configuration- and security-related setting on their accounts. In the same way, if a company has some agreement related to employee confidentiality, the employee must restrict for posting or sharing and release information about the same. To avoid the above-mentioned issues related to information leakage, you should be aware of different security settings and policies provided by different social network platform. Also, when you create a social network page in Facebook, Twitter, LinkedIn, and in other social network platforms, users should share their contact information on restricted information area. There may be some other areas in the profile page like summary box where the user can include their personal and professional details (Kumar, 2019; Bharathi & Selvarani, 2019; Li, Zhang, & Zhang, 2018; Gupta et al., 2018).

Being aware, in which way you publish the social content in your social platform, you can reduce the chance of getting affected and that impact your safety. While the features for securing your account are associated with the account, it also relates to taking various defensive solutions or precautions on the shared information. Because of this, knowing what to say and what not can help a user to protect their account information and profile content.

3.7 COBRAS (CONSUMER BRAND-RELATED ACTIVITY)

Every business personnel should use social media platform to involve people through COBRAs (consumer brand-related activity) for promotion and advertisement of their product. For this process, the users have to invite different visitors to their social media sites for posting of contents as audios or videos. A good example is how a social media platform engages different customers to show different activities related to a brand depicted in Figure 3.1. (Kaur & Singh, 2016)

FIGURE 3.1   Activities related to brand.

3.8 HASHTAG

To convert a specific topic and phrases into a clickable link to your post on your profile timeline is called hashtag that helps the different users to find their topic of choice they are interested in. When some user clicks on those links, he/she able to identify and see the forwarded post that includes ant specific hashtag (Wu & Liu, 2018). When someone uses the hashtag as a feature on their own Facebook page, they must have to follow some rules. These rules include the following:

- A hashtag always written as a single word without any spaces.
- You can include number as much required but it cannot support punctuation and special character.
- If someone wants to search the hashtag, he/she can use search bar at the top of the page.

Existing hashtag allows the social network users to interact with various users who have common interest, feelings, and similar contents. But if you talk regarding creation of campaign, you have to follow the guidelines to create net hashtag. Various methods are available for detecting hashtag that is used. The simple way is to put the hashtag on Twitter or Google to identify regarding that hashtag. The other websites like www.hashtag.org also provide information related to hashtag. The websites use the API for streaming and displayed the contents related to hashtag within 24 hours of time (Aggarwal, Rajadesingan, & Kumaraguru, 2012). One of the most popular sites called Hashtagify.org used to extract users' information quickly related to hashtag if any. Using this tool, the user of social network capable enough to extract information related to hashtag with graphical displays. It also displays various variant spellings of the one you entered, tweets, top influencer, and other age-related issues.

3.9 MISTAKE IN REPLYING TO USERS OF SOCIAL NETWORK

In social network platforms, people want to respond to a message or other posts shared by different users or from a different community. Sometimes, people need some direct answer for their posts in social network platforms. It may be that person may have some queries and other users can answer them. Conversely, it may be sometimes the users get some negative advice and information for what they want. You could also send them some direct message through email or Tweets through URLs or some blogs on a Facebook page (Journal et al., 2018). The information received or saved during exchanging information could be private and hidden from me. Similarly, on Facebook, people can comment or posts that others make a comment. It is a common practice to represent the user name at the beginning of what you have to send, as an example, if someone wants to address other users' names through making a comment on Facebook and sometimes tweet in Twitter. The visibility mode of every tweet should be set by the users for their follower and followings. Sometimes the best way to manage and handle the situation is to do nothing. Based on the follower and followings in Facebook and Twitter, people likes your content what you shared in the posts. If some people reply to a particular post in negative way, then other people also react on their comments if the posted information is true (Wang et al., 2013). If a user wants to interact with others, the dealing method with upset customer is the same as the known users too. For this process, certain things should be in your mind describes below.

- *Allow the person to escape*: Based on the user behaviour and attitude through online comment, judge the user or customer. For betterment of relation with the user, you have to follow the way they write the comment on some specific event and then reply back to the same.
- *Be adopted*: When you reply to a comment of a post, observe the issue and then comment. Understanding the point of action is the best practice for reply back. The method you follow for reply and action is the online mode. So, observation related to content description is the main point of action.
- *Way to resolve the issue*: If the user and the customer face with some issues related to your product and the service, try to resolve the issues with suitable reply back. By offering the suitable alternative, it will show how much you care for their response. The way you handle the situation will reflect a lot in other sites too.

3.10 COLLECTIVE INTELLIGENCE

When people work together as a group, it shows the intellect work and is called collective intelligence in a sociological concept. It is a better process when the people work together and solve any issues. They interact among yourself and competing with each other to resolve the issues. By this process, they cover each and every issue generated through various posts in social network platforms.

When the people find some solution to a particular question, they have the chance to select correct answers and discard all other. Collective intelligence helps the social network users a lot and provides benefit to personal user as well in organisational level. Various survey and posts are available on social network platforms called Facebook, Twitter, and LinkedIn (Humphreys, 2007) that allow you to identify different patterns and trends in people' opinions. To analyse the popularity of pattern one another, the various options like tweet, like, share, and comment help a lot. By analysing and monitoring the reaction of different users, we can follow the majority of user's preference which is trend. Another prominent social network platform called Pinterest. By uploading photos to that bookmarking site, you can also follow a certain pattern. That pattern shows on Pinboard can also be shared with others through Facebook. This process also increases the exposer of different products. While the resultant trend is not the accurate information, it nearly shows the pattern. People follow those patterns to share the product as well as various service related to them. One of the most important terms called crowdsourcing is also related to collective and collaborative effort. In this, each individual in a large group provide inputs and perform their task (Zhang, Yong, Li, Pan, & Huang, 2017). At last, all the collective entities are gathering together to complete the entire process of operation.

When the term crowdsourcing comes into picture, so does Wikipedia, i.e. the content posted by anyone can be reviewed by many others. By this process, the inaccurate information is filtered out because so many people from same background reviewed that content in a proper manner. Another crowdsourcing example is bar database. All this information helps the people regarding different opinions related to different queries. In that portal, all the information related to drink, prices, and many others can be shared with different people (Yeh, Huang, Joseph, Shieh, & Tsaur, 2012). Various public sites allow the users to work with different collaborative efforts. As an example, wikis provide various useful tools for finding public information, and they validate if the information have proper source or not.

Also, Microsoft SharePoint or yammer.com also is useful for different companies. Microsoft SharePoint has the capability to share the content through social network services instead off corporate network. Both the services mentioned earlier share files and work on different projects with various organisations without use of email services. So, by this process, the user can avoid work with multiple services (Shehnepoor, Salehi, Farahbakhsh, & Crespi, 2017). By creating new sites in Microsoft SharePoint, we can also develop wikis and that permit the members of your organisation to create knowledge-based organisation. The all these activities create a big problem in social network environment. So, the protection of user content is the most when we use all these services for knowledge sharing and other activities too.

Interaction among people — their communication and collaboration — allows the user to be a part of a more complex entity. This process gathers together the combined knowledge and experience of a group, and their collective effort gives answers, organises complex projects and predicts trends. To complete the process and getting the final goal are the main activities of the crowdsourcing and individual actions.

3.11 CONCLUSION

OSNs provide various opportunities to their users for information sharing, product advertisements and other tasks. When the user gets these opportunities, they must aware of their benefits as well as weaknesses too. To protect user information and account user must aware of what they do and what they don't. By considering the social network platform and the opportunities, this chapter highlights various opportunities that are associated with social network platform. It also highlighted how to fix the social authority, engagement of the user in OSNs, how to share the information with your friends and colleges. Finally, this chapter describes the collective intelligence and mistakes by the user when they reply to various users' comments.

REFERENCES

Aggarwal, A., Rajadesingan, A., & Kumaraguru, P. (2012). PhishAri: Automatic real-time phishing detection on twitter. *ECrime Researchers Summit, ECrime*, 1–12. https://doi.org/10.1109/eCrime.2012.6489521

Agrawal, D. P., Wang, H., Sahoo, S. R., & Gupta, B. B. (2019). Security issues and challenges in online social networks (OSNs) based on user perspective. *Computer and Cyber Security*, 591–606. https://doi.org/10.1201/9780429424878-22

Alghamdi, B., Watson, J., & Xu, Y. (2017). Toward detecting malicious links in online social networks through user behavior. *Proceedings – 2016 IEEE/WIC/ACM International Conference on Web Intelligence Workshops, WIW 2016*, 5–8. https://doi.org/10.1109/WIW.2016.41

Al-Qurishi, M., Rahman, S. M. M., Hossain, M. S., Almogren, A., Alrubaian, M., Alamri, A., & Gupta, B. B. (2018). An efficient key agreement protocol for sybil-precaution in online social networks. *Future Generation Computer Systems, 84*, 139–148.

Al-Zoubi, A. M., Alqatawna, J., & Faris, H. (2017). Spam profile detection in social networks based on public features. *2017 8th International Conference on Information and Communication Systems, ICICS 2017*. https://doi.org/10.1109/IACS.2017.7921959

Bharathi, R., & Selvarani, R. (2019). Software reliability assessment of safety critical system using computational intelligence. *International Journal of Software Science and Computational Intelligence (IJSSCI)*, *11*(3), 1–25.

Carullo, G., Castiglione, A., Cattaneo, G., De Santis, A., Fiore, U., & Palmieri, F. (2013). FeelTrust: Providing trustworthy communications in Ubiquitous Mobile environment. *Proceedings – International Conference on Advanced Information Networking and Applications, AINA*, 1113–1120. https://doi.org/10.1109/AINA.2013.100

Chaudhary, P., & Gupta, B. B. (2017). A novel framework to alleviate dissemination of XSS worms in online social network (OSN) using view segregation. *Neural Network World*, *27*, 5–25. https://doi.org/10.14311/NNW.2017.27.001

Guo, L., Zhang, C., & Fang, Y. (2015). A trust-based privacy-preserving friend recommendation Scheme for online social networks. *IEEE Transactions on Dependable and Secure Computing*, *12*(4), 413–427. doi: https://doi.org/10.1109/TDSC.2014.2355824.

Gupta, S., Gupta, B. B., & Chaudhary, P. (2018). Hunting for DOM-based XSS vulnerabilities in mobile cloud-based online social network. *Future Generation Computer Systems*, *79*, 319–336.

Gupta, B. B., Sangaiah, A. K., Nedjah, N., Yamaguchi, S., Zhang, Z., & Sheng, M. (2018). Recent research in computational intelligence paradigms into security and privacy for online social networks (OSNs). *Future Generation Computer Systems*, *86*, 851–854. https://doi.org/10.1016/j.future.2018.05.017

Humphreys, L. (2007). Mobile social networks and social practice: A case study of dodgeball. *Journal of Computer-Mediated Communication*, *13*(1), 341–360. doi: https://doi.org/10.1111/j.1083-6101.2007.00399.x.

Journal, A. I., Singh, M., Bansal, D., Sofat, S., Singh, M., Bansal, D., & Sofat, S. (2018). Who is who on Twitter – Spammer, fake or compromised account? A tool to reveal true identity in real-time who is who on Twitter – Spammer, fake or compromised. *Cybernetics and Systems*, *49*(1), 1–25. doi: https://doi.org/10.1080/01969722.2017.1412866.

Kaur, R., & Singh, S. (2016). FULL-LENGTH ARTICLE A survey of data mining and social network analysis based anomaly detection techniques. *Egyptian Informatics Journal*, *17*(2), 199–216. doi: https://doi.org/10.1016/j.eij.2015.11.004.

Kefi, H., & Perez, C.. (2018). Dark side of online social networks: Technical, managerial, and behavioral perspectives. *Encyclopedia of Social Network Analysis and Mining, January*, 1–22. https://doi.org/10.1007/978-1-4614-7163-9_110217-1

Kumar, A. (2019). Design of secure image fusion technique using cloud for privacy-preserving and copyright protection. *International Journal of Cloud Applications and Computing (IJCAC)*, *9*(3), 22–36.

Li, C., Zhang, Z., & Zhang, L. (2018). A novel authorization scheme for multimedia social networks under cloud storage method by using MA-CP-ABE. *International Journal of Cloud Applications and Computing (IJCAC)*, 8(3), 32–47.

Liang, H., Chen, Z., & Wu, J. (2018). Dynamic reputation information propagation based malicious account detection in OSNs. *Wireless Networks*, 0123456789. doi: https://doi.org/10.1007/s11276-018-1795-z.

Mateen, M., Iqbal, M. A., Aleem, M., & Islam, M. A. (2017). A hybrid approach for spam detection for Twitter. *Proceedings of 2017 14th International Bhurban Conference on Applied Sciences and Technology, IBCAST 2017*, 466–471. https://doi.org/10.1109/IBCAST.2017.7868095

Sahoo, S. R., & Gupta, B. B. (2019). Classification of various attacks and their defence mechanism in online social networks : A survey. *Enterprise Information Systems, 00*(00), 1–33. doi: https://doi.org/10.1080/17517575.2019.1605542.

Sahoo, S. R., & Gupta, B. B. (2019b). Hybrid approach for detection of malicious profiles in twitter. *Computers and Electrical Engineering, 76*, 65–81. https://doi.org/10.1016/j.compeleceng.2019.03.003

Shehnepoor, S., Salehi, M., Farahbakhsh, R., & Crespi, N. (2017). NetSpam: A network-based spam detection framework for reviews in online social media. *IEEE Transactions on Information Forensics and Security, 12*(7), 1585–1595. https://doi.org/10.1109/TIFS.2017.2675361

Sahoo, S. R., & Gupta., B. B. (2020). Classification of spammer and nonspammer content in online social network using genetic algorithm-based feature selection. *Enterprise Information Systems, 14*(5), 710–736. https://doi.org/10.1080/17517575.2020.1712742

Stergiou, C., Psannis, K. E., Xifilidis, T., Plageras, A. P., & Gupta, B. B. (2018). Security and privacy of big data for social networking services in cloud. *IEEE INFOCOM 2018-IEEE Conference on Computer Communications Workshops (INFOCOM WKSHPS)*, 438–443. IEEE.

Tous, R., Gomez, M., Poveda, J., Cruz, L., Wust, O., Makni, M., & Ayguad, E. (2018). Automated curation of brand-related social media images with deep learning. *Multimedia Tools and Applications, 77*, 27123–27142.

Wang, D., Navathe, S. B., Liu, L., Irani, D., Tamersoy, A., & Pu, C. (2013). Click traffic analysis of short URL spam on Twitter. *Proceedings of the 9th IEEE International Conference on Collaborative Computing: Networking, Applications and Worksharing, COLLABORATECOM 2013*, 250–259. https://doi.org/10.4108/icst.collaboratecom.2013.254084

Wu, L., & Liu, H. (2018). Tracing fake-news footprints: Characterizing social media messages by how they propagate. *WSDM 2018 – Proceedings of the 11th ACM International Conference on Web Search and Data Mining, 2018-Febua*, 637–645. https://doi.org/10.1145/3159652.3159677

Yeh, L. Y., Huang, Y. L., Joseph, A. D., Shieh, S. W., & Tsaur, W. J. (2012). A batch-authenticated and key agreement framework for P2P-based online social networks. *IEEE Transactions on Vehicular Technology, 61*(4), 1907–1924. doi: https://doi.org/10.1109/TVT.2012.2188821.

Zhang, B., Yong, R., Li, M., Pan, J., & Huang, J. (2017). A hybrid trust evaluation framework for E-commerce in online social network: A factor enrichment perspective. *IEEE Access, 5*, 7080–7096. https://doi.org/10.1109/ACCESS.2017.2692249

Zhu, T., Gao, H., Yang, Y., Bu, K., Chen, Y., Downey, D., Lee, K., Choudhary, A. N. (2016). Beating the artificial chaos: Fighting OSN spam using its own templates. *IEEE/ACM Transactions on Networking, 24*(6), 3856–3869. doi: https://doi.org/10.1109/TNET.2016.2557849.

Machine-Learning and Deep-Learning-Based Security Solutions for Detecting Various Attacks on OSNs

4

This chapter describes various challenges that exist in the existing state-of-the-art techniques to eradicate various threats in social network platform. It also describes how to identify various threats like fake profiles attacks using machine-learning and deep-learning-based analysis through an efficient and robust mechanism. The detection of fake profiles totally depends on its feature analysis and profile behaviour in different circumstances. Finally, this chapter also describes various strength and weaknesses of fake detection frameworks.

4.1 INTRODUCTION

Many online social network (OSN) sites provide features which enables user to subscribe to another user's profile in order to view their personal updates as posts. This process permits the social network users to follow other users in the same or in different networks (Fire, Goldschmidt, & Elovici, 2014). One of the famous social network platforms is Twitter that allows some functionalities like follower and following. Using all these features, the attacker creates fake accounts and spreads malicious information in the form of messages or news. People create some Sybil accounts and collect user credentials, which is then spread all over the network to hamper other users.

Most of the time, people create a cluster of fake accounts to collect user credentials in various ways. To gain reputation in OSNs such as in Twitter, a user also purchases followers from various websites. In current scenario, Twitter is the prominent source of information as news and advertisements (Sahoo, S. R. and Gupta, B. B., 2019). Therefore, using these credentials, various agents have gained popularity. News like earthquake, social movements, and other recent information can be circulated in this microblogging platform in a short span of time (Masood et al., 2011). In the current scenario, detection of malicious account considering those fake in a microblogging platform called Twitter is a challenging task. If one of the profiles in Twitter contains good information and more followers, it will turn out to be a popular account with reputation.

As an example, Narendra Modi is popular on Twitter with more than 45 million followers. Also, sometimes some of the fake accounts are created by computers called bots that behave similar to human-generated accounts. The basic intention of creating fake accounts is to gain the user's credentials, propagate terrorist activity, online extremism, and broadcast fake information. In some cases, the fake accounts are created to forge election results and stock market analysis (Shah, Lamba, Beutel, & Faloutsos, 2017). Various solutions and techniques are proposed by researchers and academicians for the analysis and detection of fake accounts in Twitter. These solutions solve various issues related to fake accounts. But no solution exists for the detection of source node from where the contents are generated. Moreover, all these solutions are based on the analysis of machine-learning-based solutions.

The platform for detection mechanism of fake accounts is different due to various feature analyses. Existing approaches based on graph algorithms like trust propagation, graph clustering, and graph matrix are not sufficient to detect fake accounts due to the following issues: first, all these solutions do not use traceback mechanism for detecting the source node from where these contents are generated (Al-zoubi, Faris, & Hassonah, 2018). Second, the features used for fake detection is not sufficient for the analysis of malicious contents. Therefore, there is a need for detecting fake accounts in Twitter with high true-positive rate with more features.

4.2 MOTIVATION TOWARDS WORKING

Social network platforms are totally based on the trust of the user, network services, and the service provider. Various approaches have been proposed for the detection of fake accounts on Twitter microblogging platform (Gupta, 2015). All these approaches are not sufficient for detection of fake accounts due to public feature analysis. Also, detecting the source from where the content is generated is a challenging task. Therefore, the detection of malicious content and the accounts spreading those contents is a broad area of research.

4.3 PROBLEM DEFINITION

Intruders create fake accounts for fulfilling their motives like sending malicious URLs, posts, and other messages to legitimate users to collect sensitive information, campaign management, and to increase popularity. All these activities cannot be monitored by the service provider. To analyse and detect such network in OSNs platform is tedious (Zhang, Zheng, Li, Du, & Zhu, 2014). All the existing approaches are not capable enough for detecting malicious content in the form of fake accounts. Moreover, these approaches do not use any traceback mechanism for the identification of source nodes. So, in depth, it is required to gather public as well as private information for the analysis of fake accounts.

4.4 PROPOSED APPROACH FOR FAKE-ACCOUNT DETECTION

The proposed approach detects fake accounts and informs the user with a pop-up message in the homepage. The execution of detail approach uses chrome extension and works on the dataset to separate fake and legitimate accounts depicted in Figure 4.1.

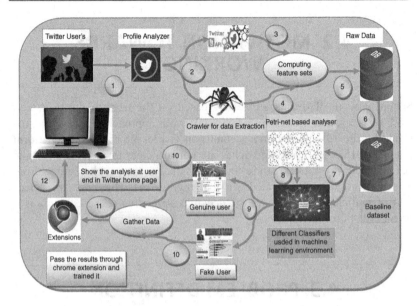

FIGURE 4.1   Proposed approach for the detection of fake profiles in Twitter.

4.5 CHARACTERISTICS ANALYSIS OF TWITTER ACCOUNTS

To classify and detect malicious account in Twitter, the analysis of features is the most prominent way. So, we analysed various characteristics based on their usage, which are describe in Table 4.1.

4.6 SELECTION OF FEATURES AND COMPUTING FEATURE SETS

To analyse a user's activity in Twitter, we have generalised different features. Existing research work performs differentiation of fake and legitimate accounts on the basis of certain characteristics associated with user's profile (Hong, Gao, Hao, & Li, 2015). For instance, legitimate users have more legitimate friends, whereas fake account holders have limited friends. Fake account holders share many videos and images with some URLs as a comment. The selections of various types of features are described in Table 4.2.

TABLE 4.1 Analysis of features on the basis of their uses

FEATURE	ANALYSIS
Tweet	Sharing of opinion and views in the form of text, image, and video is treated as Tweet in Twitter. By this process, the user of that network communicates with other users and shares their views. However, different fake users use this feature to post messages and gather user's credentials. The people who visit this malicious content will be affected eventually
Followings	The process of connecting two different accounts through Twitter is called following. When the user is following others' account, the content shared by that user is visible. When people follow, they may post some malicious links. When the user clicks on those links, the account gets affected
Followers	To gain the user's attention towards their account, fake users always follow different peoples. By using this feature, malicious account users spread malicious links and contents
Tweet with replies	The process of replying to any message is called replies with tweet. This feature allows the users to put forward their views. Malicious users spread malicious information
Media content shared	One of the most suitable features provided by Twitter for uploading images, videos, and live performance. Malicious users use this feature and propagate malicious content over the network. This feature uses various hashtags to point a specific persons or topic
Retweet (Kušen & Strembeck, 2018)	Reposting others' tweet is called retweet in Twitter. By this process, users can reply to other's messages. Most of the times, people use retweet of the fake users and give their opinion
Tagging	A user can tag a specific user in their message through the tagging feature to point at a specific user. To get more followers and increase social media engagement, the fake profile users tweet certain messages and post certain images or video to a specific user
Like	To appreciate the content shared by other users, Twitter provides the facility called like. Fake users always try to capture and attract other users by liking different content in the network
URLs	Through this feature, a fake user always sends malicious information over the network. When any user clicks on those URLs, they are redirected to different sites. Sometimes, fake account holders use short URL services for spreading malicious contents through tiny.cc and is.gd

TABLE 4.2   Selection of various features

FEATURES AND THEIR USE

VARIOUS FEATURES OF TWITTER ASSOCIATED WITH TWITTER ACCOUNT (TF)		FEATURE NUMBER
#Prof ID (tf_1)		F1
#Description (tf_2)		F2
#Date of creation (tf_3)		F3
#Protected (tf_4)		F4
#Tweet (tf_5)	#Total tweets ($tf_5 1$)	F5
	#Favorite tweets ($tf_5 2$)	
	#Avg. tweets per day ($tf_5 3$)	
	#Tweet with URLs and hashtag ($tf_5 4$)	
#Followers (tf_6)	#Total followers ($tf_6 1$)	F6
	#Total followers with direct message ($tf_6 2$)	
	#Total followers per day ($tf_6 3$)	
#Following (tf_7)	#Total followings ($tf_7 1$)	F7
	#Total followings per day ($tf_7 2$)	
# Replies on Tweet (tf_8)	#Total number of replies ($tf_8 1$)	F8
	#Average number of replies per day ($tf_8 2$)	
#Media Content (tf_9)	#Total audio content ($tf_9 1$)	F9
	#Total video content ($tf_9 2$)	
	#Content with URLs ($tf_9 3$)	
#Retweet (tf_{10})	#Total number of retweets ($tf_{10} 1$)	F10
	#Avg. number of retweets ($tf_{10} 2$)	
	#Retweet with hashtag or URLs. ($tf_{10} 3$)	
#Like (tf_{11})	# Total likes ($tf_{11} 1$)	F11
#Direct message service (tf_{12})		F12
#URLs (tf_{13})	#Total URLs ($tf_{13} 1$)	F13
	#URL's with hashtag ($tf_{13} 2$)	
#Listed count (tf_{14}) (Sahoo & Gupta, n.d.)		F14
#Verified account (tf_{15})		F15
# Background image (tf_{16})		F16
#Default profile view (tf_{17})	0(Default) 1(Changed)	F17
# Translator used (tf_{18})		F18
# Notifications (tf_{19})		F19
# Hashtags (tf_{20})	#Total number of hashtag ($tf_{20} 1$)	F20
	#Average number of hashtag ($tf_{20} 2$)	
	#Total unique hashtag ($tf_{20} 3$)	
	# Hashtag with URLs ($tf_{20} 4$)	
#Mentions (tf_{21})		F21

4.7 CONSTRUCTION OF A RAW DATASET AND THE CREATION OF A LABELLED DATASET FROM RAW DATA

To detect malicious information as fake account, a labelled dataset is required. All this information passes through chrome extension for smooth identification. By analysing public profiles, we generated label dataset from raw information. For identification, we manually labelled dataset as fake or legitimate on the basis of characteristic analysis and profile activities (Ren, Liu, & Zhao, 2012). All these profile activities are selected based on malicious information propagated through URLs and hashtags. Next we analyse the profiles of those who spread a huge number of advertisements for promoting their company and others. We also analyse their tweets, retweets, and direct message information through Petri net-based analyser (Wang, Wen, & Wu, 2015). We have examined more than 6800 Twitter profiles for the construction of our dataset, and it involves both categories of profile, fake as well as legitimate. The related information for the collected dataset is shown in Table 4.3.

4.8 PETRI NET-BASED ANALYSER

Petri net is the pictorial representation/mathematical-approaching tool for describing the behaviour of various systems. As an upcoming tool, it is used to depict flow control between objects or places. We used this tool to approach a

TABLE 4.3   Details of dataset content extracted by the crawler

DIFFERENT PROFILE PARAMETERS (FAKE + LEGITIMATE)	TOTAL NUMBER OF CONTENTS SHARED THROUGH VARIOUS SERVICES	AVERAGE NUMBER OF CONTENTS SHARED BY THE USER
Twitter profile data	6824	—
Total number of tweets	59,153,788	8668
Total number of followers	4899,493	717
Total number of followings	3439,937	504
Total number of likes	16,236,669	2377
Total number of listed count	67,976	10
Total number of URLs shared	1367	.2

network structure which describes the behaviour of each profile on Twitter and its activities in the network. It is a directed graph with initial states known as start point (M_0). The graph is the representation of different Twitter accounts in the form of Petri net. It is a directed, bipartite, and weighted (Gupta & Gupta, 2016). It consists of various nodes called user's accounts, and the transition between accounts represents friends, friends of friends, and some clusters of accounts. In this approach, each node is treated as one Twitter account with a certain condition, and every transition between the nodes are treated as an event or activity shared by the user. The transition contains certain number of inputs that show the pre- and post-condition of different events. The existence of a token with an account represents the original condition associated with that account.

Start of a transition (T) in Petri net, if the place of input, i.e. P of T is carrying a weight function i.e. W(P, T) tokens, where the weight function W(P, T) shows the transition between P and T. If the event takes place, transition is fired, otherwise not. Enabling transition (T), in firing mode, removes W(P, T) tokens from each input place P of T and adds W(P, T) tokens to each output place P of T, where W(T, P) is the transition from T to P. In between the transition, if a node does not contain any input, we called it as an independent process. In our Petri net structure, performance of each individual account is analysed using characteristics of a network (Cheng, Liu, Shen, & Yuan, 2013). Every Twitter account in a Petri net is treated as one process, and the transition 'T' among processes shows the tweets, retweets, sending malicious content in the form of URLs, and other functionalities related to Twitter account behaviour.

After approaching the Petri net service for a Twitter account, behaviour of each profile is checked that is used as a feature. If a profile user tweets some content which is visible to its followers. It can be tracked using the concept of reachability property of the Petri net approach (Wang et al., 2015). Firing of a transition by the source is reachable to every other profile which is in contact with the source. Every time the user or source of generation is traced in a log file to maintain profile activity.

4.9 SIMULATION OF PETRI NET IN PN2 ENVIRONMENT

The simulation of the proposed approach in PN2 generates a PROMELA (Process Meta language) file with .pml extension (Huang et al., 2016). The generated code is in the form of LTL (linear temporal logic) formulas, i.e. the output of different transitions using the SPIN verification tool (Agrawal, Wang, Sahoo, & Gupta, 2019) described in Section 4.4.6.3. The environment constructs various state transitions with different parameters and conditions get changed in every session of the proposed process. Generated PROMELA code describes information flow and their states during approach implementation. It defines the two different arrays, i.e. m [place] and x [transition]. Information flow is in the form of transition, which can also be displayed in the form of automata view. For every agent net in the network, one LTL formula is generated. For the transition of our agent net, the LTL formula is

```
ltl {< >((m[25]==1) && (m[29] ==1) && (m[48] ==1) &&
(m[53] ==1) && (m[65] ==1) && (m[67] ==1) && (m[68] ==1)
&& (m[81] ==1))}
```

4.10 VERIFICATION USING SPIN MODEL CHECKER

Every process definition in PROMELA is converted by SPIN into an optimised automation description that is used inside the approach checker. To verify the content generated in PROMELA, SPIN in effect computes the cross product of all transitions in the executing process. The approach checker converts generated results into a specific never claim process that describes a specific automation system and the acceptance condition of the proposed approach in the form of execution graph. Results from SPIN i.e. verification of the PML code describe the content of reachability of the tweet in the form of transmission through different transitions with initial and final points. Source and the targets are marked at every scenario in the transmission (Sahoo & Gupta, 2020). The content generated and tested using SPIN describes the effectiveness of the approach in terms of memory usage and the content generated. The code mentioned next describes the effectiveness of the content in terms of reachability of the node from source to destination.

```
:: atomic{inp2(m[33], m[81]) → x[0]=1;out2(m[59],m[88]);}
:: atomic{inp1(m[23] →x[1]=1;out1(m[4]);}
:: atomic{inp2(m[35], m[81]) → x[2]=1;out2(m[59],m[90]);}
:: atomic{inp1(m[25] →x[3]=1;out1(m[4]);}
:: atomic{inp1(m[4] →x[4]=1;out1(m[18]);}
:: atomic{inp1(m[59] →x[5]=1;out1(m[53]);}
```

4.11 EVALUATION OF RESULT AND PERFORMANCE ANALYSIS

The performance of the fake detector framework is evaluated at real time using different experimental analysis with base line dataset. The details of our experiment are mentioned in following subsections.

4.11.1 Execution Method and Result

We have used various classification approaches to conduct various experiments on the collected dataset using a machine-learning tool called WEKA (Rajput, Aharwal, Dubey, Saxena, & Raghuvanshi, 2011). To train and test the dataset, use tenfold cross-validation techniques that divide the whole dataset into 10 equal-sized subsets for the given dataset. The main aim of this method is to efficiently process our dataset to generate successful result in the form of confusion matrix. Each individual cells of confusion matrix justify the performance. The result in the form of true-positive, true-negative, false–positive, and false-negative shows the actual performance of the analysis. Also, our performance calculated sensitivity, specificity, precision, and recall value. All the evaluated results are shown in Table 4.4.

The detection system does not need any operating system-based software. Only a browser is sufficient for the execution and detection of malicious

TABLE 4.4 Classifiers output in the form of accuracy and others

				RESULTANT ANALYSIS					
DIFFERENT CLASSIFIERS	TP RATE	FP RATE	PRECISION	RECALL	F-MEASURE	MCC	ROC AREA	PRC AREA	CORRECTLY CLASSIFIED INSTANCE
Random forest	.9946	.0111	.9891	.9941	.9927	.983	.999	.999	99.16
Bagging	.9943	.0122	.9892	.9942	.9915	.982	.998	.998	99.12
JRip	.9923	.0143	.9863	.9921	.9896	.978	.991	.986	98.88
J48	.9917	.0134	.9884	.9912	.9904	.979	.991	.987	98.93
PART	.9872	.0122	.9883	.9871	.9884	.975	.993	.991	98.75
Random tree	.9854	.0173	.9842	.9851	.9846	.968	.984	.977	98.4
Logistic	.9571	.0084	.9921	.9572	.9757	.95.	.995	.995	97.4

TABLE 4.5   Flow control of the proposed fake detection framework

Algorithm 2: Predictor (using Classifier)	Algorithm 3: Predictor (for Decision Maker)
Input: A list of different feature list from the dataset ($^{tf}_1$, $^{tf}_2$............$^{tf}_{21}$)	**Input:** Feature list provided to approach
Output: Predict the output in the form of Fake or legitimate	**Output:** Decision support system in the form of value
1. Dataset← Read_Dataset (File_Path)	Predict ← Predict_using_ classifier (Features_List)
2. Approach←Random forest classifier( )	then
3. N← Fatures_List [0, 1.............N-2]	If (Predict ==1)
4. Profile-Type←Features_List [1............N-1]	Value ← "FAKE"
5. Approach.Fit (Features, Profile_Type)	else
6. Predict_Output= Approach.Predict (Features_List)	Value ← "Legitimate"

information and account. At each step, users can receive a message from the chrome extension regarding their behaviour and can then send a feedback to the service provider regarding accounts behaviour. First, when the user clicks on the chrome extension, the detection process starts, and chrome extension extracts the features of user's profile. After choosing the essential features, detection system relates profile features with other profiles for detection of clone profiles and sends the content to the server for verification. Second, at the server side, we trained our machine with random forest classifier and the extracted feature list.

Each time our server updates user information, a query is initiated with the approval of a verifier. After processing the content at server site, it displays the profile content as fake or legitimate in the form of a pop-up box at the user's home page. To optimise the classifier and to improve the accuracy of detection, feedback is collected by the user. The detection process is built with our proposed algorithm with the help of random forest classifier. The flow control mechanism of our proposed framework is depicted in Table 4.5.

4.12 CHAPTER SUMMARY

In this chapter, we have presented a fake detection framework through hybrid approach for fake Twitter profile detection and is also deployed as a Chrome extension as a service at user's homepage. This is accomplished by analysing various characteristics/features through supervised machine-learning classification techniques and identifying the source nodes that spread fake content through Petri net. Also, we have implemented our approach as a chrome extension with Petri net structure and machine-learning approaches. It has achieved more precision in detection based on our reliable data crawled from Twitter. Our approach achieved better performance with 99.169% correctly classified instances with True Positive rate of 99.46% as compared to other existing approaches. The experimental results revealed that the approach successfully deployed at user side on chrome environment is able to detect the fake accounts in real time by analysing public as well as private features.

REFERENCES

Agrawal, D. P., Wang, H., Sahoo, S. R., & Gupta, B. B. (2019). Security issues and challenges in online social networks (OSNs) based on user perspective. In *Computer and cyber security* (pp. 591–606). https://doi.org/10.1201/9780429424878-22

Al-zoubi, A. M., Faris, H., & Hassonah, M. A. (2018). Knowledge-based systems evolving support vector machines using whale optimization algorithm for spam profiles detection on online social networks in different lingual contexts. *Knowledge-Based Systems, 153*, 91–104. https://doi.org/10.1016/j.knosys.2018.04.025

Cheng, J. J., Liu, Y., Shen, B., & Yuan, W. G. (2013). An epidemic model of rumor diffusion in online social networks. *European Physical Journal B, 86*(1) 1–7. https://doi.org/10.1140/epjb/e2012-30483-5

Fire, M., Goldschmidt, R., & Elovici, Y. (2014). Online social networks: Threats and solutions. *IEEE Communications Surveys and Tutorials, 16*(4), 2019–2036. doi: https://doi.org/10.1109/COMST.2014.2321628.

Gupta, A. (2015). Improving spam detection in online social networks. *2015 International Conference on Cognitive Computing and Information Processing(CCIP)*, 1–6. https://doi.org/10.1109/CCIP.2015.7100738

Gupta, S., & Gupta, B. B. (2016). *Alleviating the proliferation of JavaScript worms from online social network in cloud platforms* (pp. 246–251).

Hong, W., Gao, Z., Hao, Y., & Li, X. (2015). A novel SCNDR rumor propagation model on online social networks. *2015 IEEE International Conference on Consumer Electronics – Taiwan, ICCE-TW 2015*, 154–155. https://doi.org/10.1109/ICCE-TW.2015.7216829

Huang, T.-K., Rahman, M. S., Madhyastha, H. V., Faloutsos, M., & Ribeiro, B. (2016). *An analysis of socware cascades in online social networks* (pp. 619–630). https://doi.org/10.1145/2488388.2488443

Kušen, E., & Strembeck, M. (2018). Why so emotional? An analysis of emotional bot-generated content on Twitter. *COMPLEXIS 2018 – Proceedings of the 3rd International Conference on Complexity, Future Information Systems and Risk, 2018-March*(Complexis), 13–22.

Masood, F., Ammad, G., Almogren, A., Abbas, A., Khattak, H. A., Ud Din, I., ... Ripeanu, M. (2011). The socialbot network: When bots socialize for fame and money. *Annual Computer Security Applications Conference (ACSAC)*, *7*(5), 93–102. doi: https://doi.org/10.1145/2076732.2076746.

Rajput, A., Aharwal, R. P., Dubey, M., Saxena, S. P., & Raghuvanshi, M. (2011). J48 and JRIP rules for e-governance data. *International Journal of Computer Science and Security*, *5*(2), 201–207.

Ren, W., Liu, Y., & Zhao, J. (2012). Provably secure information hiding via short text in social networking tools. *Tsinghua Science and Technology*, *17*(3), 225–231. doi: https://doi.org/10.1109/TST.2012.6216751.

Sahoo, S. R., & Gupta, B. B. (n.d.). *Fake profile detection in multimedia big data on online social networks. X.*

Shah, N., Lamba, H., Beutel, A., & Faloutsos, C. (2017). The many faces of link fraud. *Proceedings – IEEE International Conference on Data Mining, ICDM, 2017-Novem*, 1069–1074. https://doi.org/10.1109/ICDM.2017.140

Sahoo, S. R., & Gupta., B. B. (2020). Classification of spammer and nonspammer content in online social network using genetic algorithm-based feature selection. *Enterprise Information Systems*, *14*(5), 710–736. https://doi.org/10.1080/175175 75.2020.1712742

Wang, Z., Wen, T., & Wu, W. (2015). Modeling and simulation of rumor propagation in social networks based on Petri net theory. *ICNSC 2015 – 2015 IEEE 12th International Conference on Networking, Sensing and Control*, 492–497. https://doi.org/10.1109/ICNSC.2015.7116086

Zhang, X., Zheng, H., Li, X., Du, S., & Zhu, H. (2014). You are where you have been: Sybil detection via geo-location analysis in OSNs. *2014 IEEE Global Communications Conference, GLOBECOM 2014*, 698–703. https://doi.org/10.1109/GLOCOM.2014.7036889

Various Threats and Threat-Handling Tools

5

In social media platform, people spend much of their time to share their contents and post different pictures and videos. Through this process, the attacker tries to collect a user's credentials and hamper user's information and account. This chapter describes various threats that affect the user credentials in various social network platforms. Also, it describes the categories of threats based on the user's usage and visit. Based on the surfing of contents and pages, the threats are spread over the network. To detect the threats, various researchers and security agencies develop many solutions. Based on those, this chapter also describes the different solutions for different threats and their uses over the social network platform.

5.1 INTRODUCTION

In the current scenario, online social network and media are often seen as a big threat to the productivity of business rather than cyber security. But in some cases that assumption may change. This platform is a favourite of smooth-talking scanner for their users. Social networks like Facebook, Twitter, and LinkedIn continue to expand their business due to a greater number of users involved (Shan, Cao, Lv, Yan, & Liu, 2013). This platform brings all into such a platform that they can communicate virtually without being present physically. That helps the attacker to grow their network also. Most of the users do not have knowledge regarding the security and setting that are provided by the service provider and another third-party solution also (Zhang et al., 2017; Li, Gupta, & Metere, 2018). Taking this advantage, cyber criminals' launch various attacks to theft the user credentials and hamper their personality. Based on the threats launched for different social network platform, it is categorised into many frames. Also, the launching patterns of the threats are different based on the data content shared and visibility condition of the user content. All these threats create big trouble to the user account and their personal information also.

Sometimes attackers visit the source page of the user content and inject some malicious information. They basically use various advertisements and third-party application to launch various threats. In some cases the attacker injects some short URLs to attract the user towards malicious websites. As an example, in March 2017, a Twitter phishing attack targeted more than 10,000 employees at US Department of Defence to steal some messages according to the time magazine. The social platform, Twitter, is more vulnerable because of the retweeting facility that spreads rapidly over the network to different users in the same or in different community. Another example says that one of the employees was targeted and lost his personal information and also some official information (Singh & Sharma, 2015). After creating a Twitter account, she had clicked on a link related to vacation page and discussed what they usually do with her children on summer. The attacker collected the personal information of that employee through message service.

5.2 WHY ATTACKERS LOVE SOCIAL MEDIA PLATFORMS

Compared to other platforms for data transmission and communication like email and other popular channels, social media and networks are the best way to communicate with people. This platform is used for communication, collaboration, opinion and review, brand monitoring, entertainment, media sharing, and also for paid advertising. The usage of various services is described next:

- *Communication*: The tools used for communication are basically linked to social media platforms. These tools provide facilities like blogs and websites to communicate and interact. Also, it informs and empowers the users over social platform. People also read those blogs and reply back to the users over the same page. Other social platforms like Facebook, Twitter, Instagram, and LinkedIn enhance the way of communication and information sharing between individuals and groups.

The information like personal details, audios, videos, images, and other form of information are communicated through these platforms. Also, these platforms help the user to build a strong personal relationship with other users. The attacker uses these advantages to communicate malicious information to the individuals and to the group to collect personal information of the user and group.

- *Collaboration*: Different tools are attached with some social aspects, and we use these tools on a daily basis. The platform like Wikipedia provides the ability to know every detail to the user and also platform to update user views. The collaborative tools like social media provide the facility to upload and download files in different aspects (Gupta & Gupta, 2016).

  To get the expected outcome, different individuals and groups personalise the data to get the expected outcome in a well-defined manner. Social intruders use these upload and download facilities to spread malicious information over the network. When these contents are used by different users, they affected with different threats.

- *Opinions and reviews*: In the present scenario, people in social platform provide their views and opinion on every posts or blogs. It is just like conversation with individuals and groups. By accessing social media and network, people can reply in the form of review to any one nowadays. Through this process, the users of the social network can review any restaurant and websites according to their choice. As an example, Amazon rating and review helps the user to purchase the products. The same process is followed by the users of Facebook and Twitter. Taking the advantage of this service, various intruders try to gather personal information of the user and hamper their credentials.

- *Brand monitoring*: All the consumer brands and different companies make use of these brand tools for publishing their content over social network platforms. Not all users are aware of these tools in the social platform. The presence of this platform on social network like Facebook and Twitter helps the user a lot to publish their contents over net. It also helps in summarising the content through feedback and comments about any specific business (Tous et al., 2018).

  Using social media helps the user a lot and gathers information about people's opinions on their product, brand, and services. These tools also help the user to manage the reputation of their brands on the social platform. You also resolve the issues related to your brand by analysing the negative feedback of the customer. The attacker uses this process to spread malicious information and give negative feedback to the user's product to hamper their credentials.

- *Entertainment*: For entertainment, people play game in social media platform. Nowadays, the craze among the user for various entertainments increases. Games like Farmville and Mafia Wars are the primetime entertainment source and are played by the users through social network platform. The entertainment industry too depends on social network due to its popularity and user friendliness. There are many TV channels that promote live activities, which are shown to people in the form of advertisements, when visiting a social platform (Alghamdi, Watson, & Xu, 2017).

  Attackers use this platform to spread malicious information in the form of spammer, malware, and SQL injection attacks. These sites not only increase the communication among the user but also keep the people details. Furthermore, various movies and television channels and shows are promoted through these services. Also, people post various entertainment contents like audio and video based on their choice.

- *Paid advertising*: Nowadays, in order to attract people to their products, advertisements are the main source, which can be easily made available to customers through various social network platforms. Social media platforms like Facebook, LinkedIn, and Twitter provide you the facility to run paid advertisements on them. Based on the popularity of the product and services, people also give their feedback on those products. Also, the user can track the presence and performance of your paid advertisement and campaign.

- *Media sharing platform*: One of the prominent and reputable sites for entertainment is YouTube. More than 500 million people use this site for entertainment and information. Also, other social network sites called Vimeo helps the user for sharing media content. All these sites help the people a lot to create the various channels and have interaction with other users in the web (Singh, Bansal, & Sofat, 2018).

  Some of the sites help the users to upload and download music. Media sharing sites such as Spotify bring audio entertainment to users. Attackers send malicious information through this to users. When this feature is used, they can lose their information.

All the above usages of social media invite the attackers to do some malicious activities. Also, some of the other points are highly essential if we talk about the hackers. As part of the benefits are concerned, below-mentioned points highly invite the attackers to do malicious activities:

- *Victims are ready to click on the content*: Users are more comfortable with the social network platforms discussed previously compared to other messaging services like email. Unlike email, most of the social network platforms are not overrun by spam and other marketing messages. Most of the content that is visible on their page are from their friend, brands, advertisement, and other pages they have chosen to follow. The trust of these services is more as compared to other messaging services. This platform creates trustworthiness as well as camaraderie by which a social user is more likely to click a shared content or link than they would be if the link had arrived via an email service.
- *Two-third clicked the bait*: Most of the social network services provide the facility to share and upload content for their friends and others. Most of the time, an attacker spreads malicious contents through different links. Those links are automatically created through bots. According to the survey by ZeroFox, most of the hacker created the bots that spread automatically over the network when the user clicks on those links. He tested that, out of 100 threats, more than 66% are spread through automated bots.
- *Personal data freely available*: Social network platform provides the bunch of information about the user's credential and related information too. Depending on the security setting, information is available publicly or in private mode. Based on the security setting, an attacker might be able to gather their contacts, current location information, as well as the topic of interest. Compared with other messaging services, without breaking a person's security, a user can collect some of the information about that user (Zhang & Gupta, 2018). Also, a hacker can collect information about a specific user from other online sources. Including this, the social network platform offers the user one-step shopping on their page. Attackers also gather information, tailor different campaign, and launch it in the same or different channels.
- *Everyone in social media*: As a common platform in the form of digital communication, social media becomes a common target for cyber criminals. Due to popularity of network, people share their personal contents over the network, which helps the cyber criminals to collect information about the user and conduct malicious activities.

5.3 CATEGORIES OF SOCIAL MEDIA ATTACKS BASED ON ACCOUNT TYPES

In social media platforms, attackers use to gather personal information of the user's through various source. Attackers always look for the root to enter into a user's account and gather personal credentials. The way the attacker gathers information is based on the user's account and its type. Based on the usage and attack type, all these threats are categorised into different types. Below-mentioned example shows how these threats are affecting social network users:

- *Social media threats are surging*: The number of fake accounts is increasing day by day and growing more than 300% from Q1 to Q2 in 2019 according to the report from Proofpoint. The process of spreading malicious content through fake account is quite different from others. The attacker always tries to gather personal information of the user by sending malicious links from trusted source. But these sources are not trusted. All these accounts are created by the attacker by collecting personal information of the user from the same or different networks (Liu, Wang, Zhang, Chen, & Xiang, 2017).
- *Family member phished on Twitter*: In March 2017, one Twitter threat was detected in the form of phishing attack and targeted more than 10,000 people. One of them is an employee of US defence. Her wife operated the Twitter accounts, and through this, the attacker targeted her husband's account by sending malicious links.

5.3.1 Categories of Online Social Media Attacks

The categories of social network attacks are based on the behaviour and way of hampering the user. All these categories are described next:

- *Impersonation attack (individual)*: The impersonation attack is also called profile cloning attack. This threat uses various fake accounts to hamper other users by stealing their personal information. Through this process, the attacker sends some malicious links to the user. When the user clicks on those links, they are redirected to other pages. This process is also used to spy other account in same or in different networks. One of the examples is the Russian government that monitored and controlled the activities of different social network accounts of the French president Emmanuel Macron.

- *Impersonation attack (brand)*: In some cases, attackers try to gather information of any industries or companies by sending malicious information to the group. By this activity, the attacker creates fake accounts in the name of customer support and spreads malicious links. When a user on the same or different network complains regarding any issue, they try to offer helps and leading the victim to danger (Agrawal, Wang, Sahoo, & Gupta, 2019).

- *Manipulation*: To reach to the user and gather credential of those users, attackers try to send inflated clicks, likes, and shares through fake accounts. These activities encourage social network to prioritise these information and contents over other useful contents. Through this, the reputation of the fake account increases and the account holder easily gathers personal content.

- *Bots*: Hackers always try to get shortcut methods to gain the user credential. The process of creating bot account is one of them. Sometimes these bots are human created and sometimes controlled by the systems called system-generated bot. The bot spreads automatically when someone clicks on this first time. The bot is also known as click fraud scam. Using this, the malicious content doubled every time and spread over the same or in different networks. Most of the time, the attacker also uses this to hijack accounts and infect them. Also, to stealing user credential, this method is widely used by the attackers over social platform.

- *Reconnaissance and spying*: Nowadays huge information is available on social network platform. Based on the style of the network and account type, the information are spread by the user – information such as approximate work, working schedule, friends, contacts, family details, interest, hobbies, work history, and other details too. The intruder always tries to attack different people over the net through various ways (Varshney, Misra, & Atrey, 2017).

  One of the most dangerous attacks is called spying. By this process, the attacker always follows the user over the network. A rich profile appears prepared for the attacker to use when creating malicious messages intending to tempt the person to click or share.

- *Malicious links (phishing and malware)*: Threats like phishing and malware on online social network behave similarly due to the usage of external link. The phishing links redirect the user to a malicious website. The behaviour of the spam either impersonates a specific brand to trick the user into entering login information or attempt to harm users' credentials. Also, these threats steal personal information of the user and gather the user's credential. Similar to phishing, malware also links to a malicious website. However, these threats can alternatively encourage users to download the payload via direct messages.

✓ *Link spreading techniques*: Most of the time, these links are spread through external links and malicious websites. The information can be broadcasted through various ways:

- *Shared content*: If a user's account is hacked, the attacker uses it to spread the attack to the victims contact through shared content. This information is visible to the user account in a pop-up box. Shared content information are very dangerous for the normal users because of their awareness and system setting.
- *Comments*: An attacker always tries to inject malicious content into popular conversation, often by replaying to some comments through hashtags. This the best way for the attacker to conduct malicious activities is by replying to the specific person as well.
- *Direct message service*: It is one of the prominent features provided by the service provider to the social network users. By this feature, the user sends direct messages and reply to the other users in the same or in different networks. Basically, the user can send messages to the followers and friends in social platform.

- *Spear phishing and tailored attacks*: One of the most sophisticated ways of cyberattack is called spear phishing attack. This type of attack can be done in every channel in social network platforms to hamper user credentials and account information. The hackers are improving the way of hacking using various tactics. They create a link cloaking principle to spread malicious information as links (Williams, Hinds, & Joinson, 2018).

5.4 CYBER SECURITY TOOLS FOR PROTECTING USER ACCOUNT AND INFORMATION

To protect user account and information in social network platforms, many levels of solutions are required. All these solutions work in different environment for protecting user information and their accounts. The types of tools and their features are described next:

- *Network security monitoring tools*: The network security and monitoring tool should have the complete visibility over all network activities and various profiles are connected. Without complete protection the threats remain undetected. Some tools are available that cannot fulfil the user's requirement due to the lack of necessary mechanism; for example if the software provides the statistical information about the flow control and do not have the idea regarding the content flow inside the network packets. Also, agent-based tools to monitor network security also have their fallings.

- *Encryption tools*: To make the system information unreadable, encryption technique is used. By this process only, the authorised person can view the content. People and devices can be authorised to access encrypted content in many ways. Some of the encryption techniques are isolated, though some encryption technique exists to protect the content by encrypting the contents. Social media communication platforms provide many security mechanisms to protect user content through encrypted contents. Tools like Tor, KeePass, and TrueCrypt help the user to encrypt their content and protect from various threats.

- *Network defence wireless tools*: Some of the network security–monitoring tools are available to protect the user content. In social network, daily new security threats appear. The progressive nature of these threats extensively damages the account and the information. This principle required multipoint security solutions. The critical administrator quickly identifies these threats to protect user content over the network. Some of the network-monitoring tools like Argus, Pof, Nagios, Splunk, and OSSEC help a lot to protect user's content from various threats.

- *Packet sniffers*: Packer sniffer work by capturing traffic data as it passes through wired and wireless medium and transfer the content into a file. Some times this is also known as packet capture. While computer systems are generally designed to ignore the noise of traffic, packet sniffer is just the opposite. This tool allows you to collect all the relevant information that are transmitted from source and destination.

- *Antivirus software*: In social media platforms, antivirus software helps the user by protecting from unauthorised access of information. It protects from phishing and spammers over the network. Antivirus like total defence security will work overtime to detect and delete malicious posts and also fix the issues to protect the devices. These products are basically for people who use different social media prominently. A result of this could be opening their computers to potential security issues.

- *Firewall*: Firewall services are used for network security system to monitor the traffic flow based on the set rules. Social media platforms are protected trough firewall services also. It establishes a barrier between user information and the channel used for communication. Firewall is just like a trade-off. The more you set the security, the more you protect. To prevent the users from unauthorised access, firewall security is the first phase. It protects the account from external access links (Lv & Zhang, 2016).
- *PKI services*: It makes authentication service and transfer of data along with online signalling convenient and secure. Various services like sign, sign hash, repository assistant, encryption, and decryption make it easier for the applicant. All these processes gather user's information, registration, and validity details related to a specific account. The security PKI works as validity details related to the usage of social network services. The basic idea of imposing this security is to make transitions secured between one or more trusted parties.
- *Managed detection and response services (MDR)*: It is a type of advanced security service that provides threat intelligence, threat hunting, security monitoring, various incident analyses, and response services also. This is similar to the Managed Security service provider (MSSPs) services that only provide some alert. Compared to other techniques and services, MDR provides deeper level of security related to endpoints, behaviour of the user, application, and network. For faster response, MDR also uses artificial intelligence and machine-learning platform to investigate various accounts in social network platform.

5.5 CHAPTER SUMMARY

In this chapter, we discuss various threats that hamper user credential in social network platform. Based on the categories of threats, we mention the way by which those threats are propagated and hamper the users. We also categorise the threats into different subgroups. Furthermore, we discuss why the attacker choose social media platform to hamper user account and steal personal information of the user. Finally, we discuss, various threats handling tools and software's. Through these tools the user can protect their account and account contents. By considering social media platform, we mentioned various threat-handling and network-handling tools that protect the user credential in various ways.

REFERENCES

Agrawal, D. P., Wang, H., Sahoo, S. R., & Gupta, B. B. (2019). Security issues and challenges in online social networks (OSNs) based on user perspective. *Computer and Cyber Security*, 591–606. https://doi.org/10.1201/9780429424878-22

Alghamdi, B., Watson, J., & Xu, Y. (2017). Toward detecting malicious links in online social networks through user behavior. *Proceedings – 2016 IEEE/WIC/ACM International Conference on Web Intelligence Workshops, WIW 2016*, 5–8. https://doi.org/10.1109/WIW.2016.41

Gupta, B. B., & Gupta, A. (2018). Assessment of honeypots: Issues, challenges and future directions. *International Journal of Cloud Applications and Computing (IJCAC)*, 8(1), 21–54.

Gupta, S., & Gupta, B. B. (2016). Alleviating the proliferation of JavaScript worms from online social network in cloud platforms. *In 2016 7th International Conference on Information and Communication Systems (ICICS)* (pp. 246–251). IEEE.

Li, T., Gupta, B. B., & Metere, R. (2018). Socially-conforming cooperative computation in cloud networks. *Journal of Parallel and Distributed Computing, 117*, 274–280.

Liu, S., Wang, Y., Zhang, J., Chen, C., & Xiang, Y. (2017). Addressing the class imbalance problem in Twitter spam detection using ensemble learning. *Computers and Security, 69*, 35–49. https://doi.org/10.1016/j.cose.2016.12.004

Lv, P., & Zhang, J. (2016). *A social network graphics segmentation algorithm based on community-detection* (pp. 619–623).

Shan, Z., Cao, H., Lv, J., Yan, C., & Liu, A. (2013). *Enhancing and identifying cloning attacks in online social networks*. 5, 1–6. https://doi.org/10.1145/2448556.2448615

Singh, M., Bansal, D., & Sofat, S. (2018). Who is who on Twitter–Spammer, fake or compromised account? A tool to reveal true identity in Real-time. *Cybernetics and Systems*, 49(1), 1–25. doi: https://doi.org/10.1080/01969722.2017.1412866.

Singh, R., & Sharma, T. P. (2015). On the IEEE 802. 11i security : A denial-of-service perspective. *August 2014*, 1378–1407. https://doi.org/10.1002/sec

Tous, R., Gomez, M., Poveda, J., Cruz, L., Wust, O., Makni, M., Ayguad, E. (2018). Automated curation of brand-related social media images with deep learning. *Multimedia Tools and Applications, 77*, 27123–27142.

Varshney, G., Misra, M., & Atrey, P. K. (2017). Detecting spying and fraud browser extensions. *MPS 2017 – Proceedings of the 2017 Workshop on Multimedia Privacy and Security, Co-Located with CCS 2017, 2017-January*, 45–52. https://doi.org/10.1145/3137616.3137619

Wang, R., Lv, M., Wu, Z., Li, Y., & Xu, Y. (2019). Fast graph centrality computation via sampling: A case study of influence maximisation over OSNs. *International Journal of High Performance Computing and Networking, 14*(1), 92–101.

Wang, G., Park, J., Sandhu, R., Wang, J., & Gui, X. (2019). Dynamic trust evaluation model based on bidding and multi-attributes for social networks. *International Journal of High Performance Computing and Networking, 13*(4), 436–454.

Williams, E. J., Hinds, J., & Joinson, A. N. (2018). Exploring susceptibility to phishing in the workplace. *International Journal of Human Computer Studies, 120*(July), 1–13. doi: https://doi.org/10.1016/j.ijhcs.2018.06.004.

Zhang, Z., & Gupta, B. B. (2018). Social media security and trustworthiness: Overview and new direction. *Future Generation Computer Systems, 86*, 914–925.

Zhang, Z., Sun, R., Zhao, C., Wang, J., Chang, C. K., & Gupta, B. B. (2017). CyVOD: A novel trinity multimedia social network scheme. *Mu6ltimedia Tools and Applications, 76*(18), 18513–18529.

Preventive Measures and General Practices

6

The statement – prevention is better than cure – is also appropriate for social network users. When the users use social network platforms for information sharing and communicating with others or belongings, security of the profile must require to protect the information and account. By considering the scenario, this chapter describes various practice tics that are required to protect the user account and information from various threats. Also, this chapter highlights some open issues and challenges in existing security solutions. Furthermore, it also highlights various principles that must be followed by the social network users to be secure. Based on the principles, users must set their accounts in such a way that no one can hamper their contents through various attacks.

6.1 INTRODUCTION

Online social network (OSN) users suffer from the major threats like fake profile attacks, spammer attack, malwares, and many others. Usually, in these attacks, the attackers steal user's credentials, spread malware, spread malicious links, fraudulent reviews, and share undesired or excessive contents and bulk messages. All these activities degrade the performance of users account and hamper their reputation (Zhang, Jing, Wang, Choo, & Gupta, 2020). By this, the attacker can lure the OSN users or audience by sharing attractive posts such as a short phrase associated with the links, saucy videos or something fluffy. Another common technique used by the attacker is the phishing attack, in which the attackers try to steal the user's credentials such as password and credit card details. Therefore, it is an important challenge to secure the user credentials from different threats.

6.2 PRACTICE TIPS TO PROTECT YOUR SYSTEM, ACCOUNT, AND INFORMATION

Apart from using different methods, framework, and architecture for protecting threats against online social networking attacks, people should be aware of certain practice and tips to protect the system and personal information from unauthorised access and attack (Alweshah et al., 2020). Some of the practice and tips that are much more beneficial to the user perspective are described below.

- *Behave like puzzled*: Online social networking is the best source for business communication and passing information in the current scenario. People share current news, events and activities by using an OSN for spreading news. Simultaneously, attackers spread certain malicious content or ineffective information in the network. It is best not to believe everything that is available on the site. Before clicking on that news or event, check the message properly using different sources. Sometimes, when the users click on that activity, some malicious software is downloaded automatically in your system.
- *Security and privacy settings*: Every online social networking site has its own privacy and security settings to protect their site and user activity. Before using the site, the users should check the security settings properly. Some social networking sites may guide you to install the software. Some services crack the ability to confine your security setting for a different activity like sharing of pictures with others and allowing you to share different contents (Al-Nawasrah, Almomani, Atawneh, & Alauthman, 2020; Kaushik & Gandhi, 2019; Olakanmi & Dada, 2019).
- *Strong passwords*: The users should apply proper, strong passwords. Do not use a password which is relevant to personal details such as date of birth or its consecutive numbers. If possible, the password should be a combination of special characters, symbols, alphabets, and numbers (Gupta & Chaudhary, 2020). To remember the passwords, always try to put a password hint or use some password management utility to store the password securely. Try to avoid simple passwords like your name, date of birth, or others that can easily

be imagined by someone. In many cases, attackers reckon the password from the information available publicly in the network.

- *Secure your password*: We should not disclose our passwords to others. Before entering your password, check the site properly. In some cases, a duplicate copy of that site is created by an attacker spreading in the form of a phishing scam. It is also called cloning attack or fake profile attack. Check the original source of the web page before doing any kind of operation or putting your information. Frequently changing the password is a good habit which uses a clean computer to log into the original server.

- *Always be attentive*: Before posing any information related to you on online social networking site, think twice. After posting personal information, it is no longer certain where the message is and who can access it in the network. This might cause personal harassment in the future. People post too much information on the web like personal information, phone number, location, etc. For forwarding virus, some people continuously post certain news, events, and location update. When the user tries to visit that link, some malicious programme is automatically downloaded.

- *Always be suspicious*: Some profiles of the people on the Internet are not what they look like. The people you follow on the social networking site might just be another fan or some other personnel. To collect information about the person or office details, some attackers create an account just like their friend (Al-Sharif, Al-Saleh, Alawneh, Jararweh, & Gupta, 2020). Before accepting any friend request, check the profile details and mutual friends too.

- *Timely updates*: Check whether the software you used is updated one or not. If it is not updated, update it. Try to update the browser, operating system, and the third-party plug-in like adobe, media player, antivirus, and other software. Try to install all the patch file of the software from the original source.

6.3 OPEN ISSUES AND CHALLENGES IN EXISTING SECURITY SOLUTIONS

The widespread use of OSNs requires some standard levels of security and threat detection mechanism. There are various issues and research challenges related to detection and mitigation of various threats in OSN. However, OSNs are still lacking with some security mechanism at users' end. In order to ensure standard quality of service in OSNs environment, suitable threat detection approaches are required which ensure proper security at users' homepage and detect malicious contents in the form of spammer. In addition, proper extension-based services are also required to detect the threats and fraudulent contents at real time. However, there are some challenges that exist in present solutions, as described below:

- *Analysis of profiles based on public and private features*: For detecting malicious content such as spammer, fraudulent news in social network platforms, various researchers use publicly available user profile features. But all these features are not sufficient to analyse and detect malicious content. Moreover, to increase the detection rate based on features analysis, public and private features of the user account are required (Bodin, García, & Robins, 2020). Therefore, while threats analyse the accounts and their contents for the purpose of threat detection, the selection of both public and private information is highly essential.

- *Identification of source node of disseminating malicious content*: Information on social network spread faster as compared to other messenger services. Fraudulent content is spread on OSNs by users through circulation of the message on friends. However, to increase the threat detection rate in OSNs, the identification of source node from where these messages are generated is highly essential. Therefore, to detect various threats in OSNs, including the identification of source node, is a challenging task.

- *Optimal features selection for better analysis of spammer content*: Analysis of spammer in social network by analysing various features is a tedious job. Manual approach of features selection leads to low true-positive rate. Moreover, better selection of appropriate features that identify spammer content in OSN is essential. Therefore, the solution of appropriate techniques for suitable feature selections and analysis the spammer activities in a reactive manner is highly essential.

- *Content-based identification of malicious information*: Malicious content detection, based on the priority of content shared and communicated by the users on OSNs is a challenging task. However, we observed that the percentage of spammer content is more in product advertisement posts as compared to other contents shared over the network by various users (Gupta, Sahoo, Chugh, Iota, & Shukla, 2020; Hewitt & Kaluzny, 2020). In order to represent and analyse the flow control of overall activities of the user on social network, there is a need for popularity-based malicious content approach which can identify various threats.

- *Processing of structured and unstructured data in a single platform*: Analysis of user contents in social network, based on extracted information and using machine learning algorithm, is a structured data processing activity. But, in many cases, filtering of unwanted information from big data is very difficult. Therefore, it requires a common platform through which the structured and unstructured data can be processed simultaneously for better analysis of malicious content.

- *Image-based spammer analysis*: Analysis of spammer through analysing images is a tedious job. However, it has been observed that the spammers spread on social network through images based on hyperlinks. But very less attention has been paid towards the detection of image-based spammer content on OSN platforms.

- *Overfitting condition and longer training time*: Implementation of user content in machine learning environment to detect various threats needs a suitable feature selection and trained dataset. But, in most of the cases, the trained data suffer from overfitting condition. Therefore, there is a need for balance dataset for classification task in machine learning environment for better decision-making and increased with desirable true-positive rate.

6.4 PRINCIPLES TO PROTECT THE USER ACCOUNT ON A SOCIAL PLATFORM

To secure the user account from unauthorised access and visit, user must aware some principles that can help a lot to the user over social network platforms. All these principles are described below.

- *Identify the community you are attached with*: To identify the community details is highly essential for the social network users if you want to shoot in a dark and to detect the attackers who can theft essential details. All these details must be identified at the first stage i.e. brainstorming (Sánchez-Mercado et al., 2020). All these networks are created to meet certain peoples and broadcast messages with known and unknown. To know the community you attached helps a lot to identifying community and number of dislikes. All these issues help you to understand the psychological factors that affect the consumer credentials. Sometimes, a little helps a lot to understand the behaviour of the account and the content associated with.

- *Define all the feature and their function*: The use of feature and function creates a big role in the profile monitoring to track every incoming and outgoing contents which are maintained in a log to protect the user account from unauthorised access. That also linked with various communities the user involved with. The requirement of those community-based contents helps the user but sometimes hampers the user accounts. The content filtration is required at every stage to protect user credentials. The overall objective of this feature is to how efficiently the content can transfer from source to destination and in protected mode. Also, it shows what type of data is shared through the channel, categories of users, and different administrative functions.

- *Choosing of the right technology for different accounts*: Before creating an account in social media platform, you have to identify the different functions and features. All the features and functions determine the platform and the purpose of creation of account. The main problem for creating your network and the connection is how transparent your account is, because the attacker always tries to enter to people's accounts to steal personal information from the user. The professionals select the appropriate technologies for their social media connection. Most of the time proper guidance is needed for securing your account and the information. If you set the security setting by yourself, you must have proper knowledge regarding that. By this process, the account will be secure and you save the time and money as well.

  Lastly, you should analyse all the information and account before creating your social network community and sharing of information. This process helps a lot to the user to protect your account from various issues. Also we mentioned other useful tips for choosing social media network and the community.

- *The structure of user account*: Once the users created their account on different social network platforms, they must go through with different security solutions. Some of the general rules must be applied by the users for building their accounts and the content shared by them. All these things are highly essential due to information sharing and public platform for communication. To manage the account, the user must follow certain rules that help the user to protect their account. To portable your account and the customer relation, below-mentioned points help the user a lot.

- *Customer service*: One of the main platforms is customer service through social network platforms. Through this the users can resolve all the technical issues.
- *Security of user account and network*: Before adding the accounts to your follower and following list, you have to check the proper security principles related to the account.
- *Scalability*: When you create a social network account and connect with people to communicate over it, you have to create the activity stream. All these networks extend a lot and manage everything through that network.
- *Designing of activity stream*: Activity stream is the core part of the social network platforms when you use social network for communication and information exchange. At first, Facebook introduced this feature for their users. This concept affects everyone in Facebook platform for their popularity. In real life, fascinating people interact with their friends and family members directly. The main objective of this feature is to know the activity and feeling of every user at every stage.

  It improves the quality of use and sharing of information platform a lot through attractive principle. Through this process, the user can send attractive activities to other users. Social network developers use Joomla and Drupal for developing activity stream because it creates some security platform for their users. As an example, activity feed of platform Ning allows the user to connect to Facebook and Twitter. These features allow the user to use like, share, and comment that shown in your news feed. The users also publish their content using tweet, post and also decide the activity shown to the user. All these features customised the user account in social network platforms.
- *Feature to update status*: It is highly essential to update the status. Every user on social network platforms updates their feelings and thoughts freely at any instance of time. The tools help a user to update their feelings and emotions over the social platforms and get notification to every user those who associated with. In current scenario, Facebook popularised with active steam. Also, Twitter made the status update to every user. Status update is the main feature

used by the user every day to contact and to attract users towards their profile. If this feature is not helpful to the user, it means the usefulness of that feature is unaware by the user. One of the most secure and balanced features of the Twitter is to restrict the user upto140 character. Also, the comment adding feature also helps the user to put their comments inside the status update. There are a lot of microblogging platforms to communicate between people virtually. Whatever the platform it may be, security must require to protect the user content from unauthorised access. All these networks use content management principle to protect the user content.

- *Qualitative view of data*: By crating attractive pages, the social network users attract many people towards their account. The social network platforms provide the facility like multiple data viewing features that increases the visibly and clarity. The various data viewing options are listed below:
  ✓ Upcoming stories
  ✓ Stories uploaded in the last 24 hours
  ✓ Stories uploaded in the last week
  ✓ Stories uploaded in the last month
  ✓ Popular stories in last year etc.

  Remember, when the social network platforms like Facebook launched their timeline features, it attracts many users towards their platform. But all these features invite the attacker to conduct some malicious activity over the Internet. Using just one click, the user got the information related to history and others. The same feature highlighted the publicity and awareness over the user.

- *Connect with right user*: After all the connection is set related to your account, the main activities start i.e. linking of account with others. When people use social network platforms for information sharing and posting of content over the network, they must aware about their friends. Those who are connected to their account must be trusted one. There are a lot of tools that help the user to identify about the user and their activity. Before accepting a friend request of others, the user must have the idea about those users in detail. Social network like Facebook created in a college environment but due to its popularity, it is now a pioneer in the social platform. Facebook also provides many security features to both individual users and for industrial application accounts. Although it is a traditional marketing platform and message communication medium, the attacker takes this advantage to do some malicious activity (Dong, Gao,

Guo, Li, & Cui, 2020). The digital marketing platform also included normal message communication medium due to its popularity. The social network platforms also provide the facility to reach your goal by setting different options mentioned below.

- *Marketing through email*: Now a day, people get some information from various parties like email services. That helps a lot to the user to reach directly to the user within a fraction of second. Secure platform provides the information related to the user and the customers too. Attackers take this advantage to gather information about the user.

- *Blogging*: Through blog service, the user discusses their new posts and other services. Different users always like to read useful information post through the social platform. They must aware about the content what he posts and likes too (Sahoo & Gupta, 2020). Through this service, different users get closer to the account and steal personal information. The user must monitor the content regularly to protect their account and the information flow.

- *Interaction with peoples*: When some person or account holder writes or posts some materials over the net, you must react and reply to their messages. Through this process, you can control the spreading of malicious news about the account (Radionova-Girsa, 2019), make a healthy connection, and build social relationship but in a fair manner. Appreciate the content if you like or reply a suitable message to those posts. But the attacker always replies some suitable messages for every post that shared through their network.

6.5 CHAPTER SUMMARY

In this chapter, we have attempted to present various practice tips for the users to protect their accounts, information, and the contents shared in social network platforms. Nevertheless, individually, each technique is less effective for the detection of various threats in social network platforms. To remain more secure and careful about the different threats, there is a requirement of multiple preventive tips integrating with each solution provided through various researchers and academicians and also multiple techniques like secure coding, static and dynamic testing of the web applications, proper filtering and sanitisation schemes, etc. In addition, we have discussed about various open issues and principles that help the user to create a new platform to protect their contents.

REFERENCES

Al-Nawasrah, A., Almomani, A. A., Atawneh, S., & Alauthman, M. (2020). A survey of fast flux botnet detection with fast flux Cloud computing. *International Journal of Cloud Applications and Computing (IJCAC)*, *10*(3), 17–53.

Al-Sharif, Z. A., Al-Saleh, M. I., Alawneh, L. M., Jararweh, Y. I., & Gupta, B. (2020). Live forensics of software attacks on cyber–physical systems. *Future Generation Computer Systems*, *108*, 1217–1229.

Alweshah, M., Al Khalaileh, S., Gupta, B. B., Almomani, A., Hammouri, A. I., & Al-Betar, M. A. (2020). The monarch butterfly optimization algorithm for solving feature selection problems. *Neural Computing and Applications*, 1–15.

Bodin, Ö, García, M. M., & Robins, G. (2020). Reconciling conflict and cooperation in environmental governance: A social network perspective. *Annual Review of Environment and Resources*, *45*.

Dong, X., Gao, C., Guo, C., Li, W., & Cui, L. (2020). Time course of attentional bias in social anxiety: The effects of spatial frequencies and individual threats. *Psychophysiology*, e13617.

Gupta, B. B., & Chaudhary, P. (2020). *Cross-site scripting attacks: Classification, attack, and countermeasures*. CRC Press.

Gupta, B. B., Sahoo, S. R., Chugh, P., Iota, V., & Shukla, A. (2020). Defending multimedia content embedded in online social networks (OSNs) using digital watermarking. In *Handbook of research on multimedia cyber security* (pp. 90–113). IGI Global.

Hewitt, A. J., Kaluzny, J. R., Rambo, D. C., Trudeau, S. M., Hall, B., & Garner, I. V., A. J. (2020). *U.S. patent no. 10,616,247*. Washington, DC: U.S. Patent and Trademark Office.

Kaushik, S., & Gandhi, C. (2019). Ensure hierarchal identity based data security in Cloud environment. *International Journal of Cloud Applications and Computing (IJCAC)*, *9*(4), 21–36.

Olakanmi, O. O., & Dada, A. (2019). An efficient privacy-preserving approach for secure verifiable outsourced computing on untrusted platforms. *International Journal of Cloud Applications and Computing (IJCAC)*, *9*(2), 79–98.

Radionova-Girsa, E. (2019, April). Threats for women in cyberspace: Be protected using Internet. *International conference on gender research* (pp. 742–748). Academic Conferences International Limited.

Sahoo, S. R., & Gupta, B. B. (2020). Popularity-based detection of malicious content in Facebook using machine learning approach. In *First international conference on sustainable technologies for computational intelligence* (pp. 163–176). Singapore: Springer.

Sahoo, S. R., & Gupta, B. B. Real-time detection of fake account in twitter using machine-learning approach. In *Advances in computational intelligence and communication technology* (pp. 149–159). Springer, Singapore.

Sánchez-Mercado, A., Urdaneta, A., Moran, L., Ovalle, L., Arvelo, M. Á., & Campos, J., ... & Rodríguez-Clark, K. M. (2020). Social network analysis reveals specialized trade in an endangered songbird. *Animal Conservation, 23*(2), 132–144.

Zhang, Z., Jing, J., Wang, X., Choo, K. K. R., & Gupta, B. B. (2020). A crowdsourcing method for online social networks security assessment based on human-centric computing. *Human-centric Computing and Information Sciences, 10*(1), 1–19.

Data Theft in Indonesia

7

A Case Study on Facebook

The fundamental rights known as right to privacy should be protected. Ironically, this is consciously carried publicly in online social network. Currently, Facebook is the largest social media with more than 2.5 billion users and they store their private information in Facebook server. In April 2018, more than 1 million data of Facebook users were stolen in Indonesia through other parties. The owner of Facebook, Mark Zuckerberg, admitted that the Facebook data of Indonesian user had been stolen by the users of other parties for their benefit. For this issue, the Indonesian Government circulated a warning letter to the Facebook owner and required clarification regarding those cases. It also shows how the Government's seriousness for the protection of personal information of its citizen is still a question. The Government of Indonesia took a bold step to protect their citizens' account information by using the protection rights of International Instrument and Indonesian legal Instruments on the protection of private rights. This section would give a proper explanation about what the Government of Indonesia should do to take a hold of this situation. To protect the public information socialisation is required towards Indonesian society should be done from the bottom to top level.

7.1 INTRODUCTION

Year after year, the information technology has spread far and wide in Indonesia. The harmony between the information technology and media has resulted in a growing variety of social services virtually. The use of social platform and Internet in various fields makes things easier. One of the legal issues which sometimes occur is the protection of user's rights by a user on his or her privacy (Asih Antika, 2018). The right to privacy refers to the rights used by a professional to protect their rights. Some of the researchers or experts express this understanding of the right to privacy. The way of communication between people and the forwarded content must be through some guidelines. The extent of privacy coverage usually makes the number of privacy setting at different levels.

The international legal instrument, freedom of privacy, is recognised as a basic right to every users of the Internet. All these provisions are a part of Universal Declaration of Human Rights (UDHR). These declarations have provided legal power to its user to protect user information. All these are present in Articles 3 and 17 of UDHR. All these protections are based on the two classes of protection – first, civil and political rights and second, protection of economy, cultural, and social rights. This is also called ECOSOC. One of the best rules of law and its obligation is one of the positive movements of its citizens. Peoples maintained all these rules regularly. This was done so that the citizens of Indonesia do not feel anxious that their personal data might be used or known to other users that he does not desire (Prosser, 2012). For an example, the personal data of Indonesian user utilised by Cambridge Analytica to reach 87 million people on social network platform called Facebook. The incident of data theft took place from the Facebook Corporation and one of the applications called 'thisisyourdigitallife.' At a survey, it came into picture that more than 748 users have installed the same application from 2013 to 2015. By this application, more than 1 million people got affected and lost their information. More than 1.26% people got affected through this incidence according to Facebook analysis.

The various rules like Regulation 20 and Article 17 are outlined in a ministerial regulation. In this rule it is mentioned that the personal data can also be used for the protection of the user's personal information in an electronic way (Yusuf, 2018). The owner of the account, who is only allowed to access the privacy of his data, has a right to lodge a complaint in order to settle a private information. Though the rule imposed in Indonesia for protecting a user's personal information is not sufficient, it is highly essential to create and impose the personal data protection law in Indonesia to protect user's information and account in Facebook or in another social network platform.

Based on the previous concern, the first issue to be described in this chapter is the extension of rules and regulations in Indonesia to protect the user's account and information. Next we explain how the Indonesian Government take certain policies and steps to provide privacy and data-protection mechanisms.

7.2 FACEBOOK DATA BREAKER IN INDONESIA

In the year 2013, one of the researchers of Cambridge University, Aleksandr Kogan, created a quiz app called 'thisisyourdigitallife.' This app is used by more than 3 Lakh people who are interested to share their personal information. Also, some of the users share their friend's data using this app (Ayuwuragil, 2018). After this, Facebook changed their data sharing policies and accessibility. According to the new policy, the developer of the app will have no access to any information from his/her friend. For that the friends of the user must have to download the app on his/her system.

After 2 years, Facebook got information from the media that Kogan has shared theses data to Cambridge Analytica by violating the principle of Facebook's policies. For this issue, the platform removed this app from their environment. But the Cambridge Analytics did not delete all the data as they had promised before. At the later stage, Facebook took action against Cambridge Analytics and removed all these services. Later the Cambridge Analytics agreed to delete all these information and to be gone with forensic proof. But the misuse of information by Kogan is widely cited as the largest data theft. As per Facebook, the theft information had spread over more than 90 million people.

7.2.1 Expert Opinion Regarding the Data Leak Case

One of the experts in cyber security, Pradama Persadha, from the Security Research Institute of Cyber and Communication from Indonesia analysed the threats related to Facebook. He reveals that the data leakage involves more than 1 million social network users in Indonesia. This is due to low security platform set by the government of Indonesia. Facebook Indonesia is still searching threats related to data leak and promise to conduct internal audit before investigation was completed. This promise has previously been conveyed by representatives of Facebook Indonesia in a public meeting for an hour by the representatives on April 2016 (http://www.australiaplus.com/indonesian/berita/fb-indonesia-dibareskrim/9674954). As a result, the house gives 1-month time to Facebook to submit its internal audit result. This result will be used to analyse the data theft issues suing potential hazards.

At the same time, he said discussing the matter with the Facebook manager in Indonesia would not have a significant impact on the settlement and follow-up in this case because Indonesia does not have the power to bargain with Facebook to follow the rules of Government. On the contrary, this point is the momentum for Indonesia to work for security principles on social media platform to protect user information and account. Same as China exemplifying Google to operate in their country and run all these using the microblogging platform Called Weibo. But the Indonesian Government admitted that there are still some security issues that exist. For now, the government is only trying to protect the user information from unauthorised access and data leak too.

7.2.2 NGO Comments on the Privacy Issues

According to the Chairman of Cyber Law Centre, Faculty of Law Padjadjaran University, stated that the protection of personal information regulation increases day by day. This leads to protect the information as well as increases the usage of Internet in Indonesia. It also enhances the sustainability of digital economy in future. The deputy director of ELSAM supports Sinta Dewi's opinion citing the resources adapted by the UN General Assembly pointing to Article 19 of the Covenant on Civil and politics (Antara, 2018). The statement describes that the protection of people those who are use on-line platform and may in off-line mode.

By considering both these cases, UN encourages state members to revise the policies related to Internet. According to the professor Wahyudi Djafar, Facebook case in Indonesia needs some analysis through data engineering rather than in line with the protection of citizens based on the usage of Internet. If it persists, the same will be continued by affecting the preferences of the online social media users with the penalties of without the rights of individual citizens. Even if he asked the Parliament to create laws for the PDP in the 2018–2019 national legislation (Sahoo & Gupta, 2020), according to him, at the time of hearing, no one will be against the establishment of that Law, so there is no reason to postpone the house.

It is not the right to block Facebook application in Indonesia due to misuse of users by the third party for data theft according to the Institute for Policy Research and advocacy. It is better to identify which data are leak, what data have been transfer, and what exactly are the violation by audits with Government and Facebook. The main issue of blocking the services always depends on the government policy and regulation. If there is no right reason, then shutdown of the application is unnecessary, otherwise it violates the principle of Facebook application. In addition to the joint audit, the government of Indonesia processes one recovery mechanism against Facebook users who deviate to follow the rules. Compensation money is also charged to Facebook with updating terms and services.

It is a better practice by the user to alienation or misuse of data will not happen again in future. Some shot of education also provided by the Facebook to handle properly the account in future. By looking to the above cases, Elsam sees the importance of human rights on various development processes. Human rights are formulated in the form of legal instrument to protect public information. To protect people's private rights, normative forms are important (Dahiya & Gupta, 2020). By this process, it ensures technological and machinery work along with artificial intelligence for various benefits of users like data collection, information exchange, and many more with protection.

It is concluded that the government of Indonesia has done various protective measures to protect user information in Facebook. The law implicitly provides privacy in a guaranteed manner. In the level of legislation, the legal regulation has not been properly outlined.

7.2.3 Government Undertook Measures

The Minister of Communication and Informatics of Indonesia said his cross care escorting the energy to hold Facebook accountable. Because, the ministerial staff says it may affect through Facebook accountable in upcoming election. The government of Indonesia had sent an explanation letter to Facebook regarding data theft and its prevention. The Government also suggested to stop using the applications related to Facebook application and all accessibilities. Same way, the company should not submit any information directly to the account owner to actively disable the content (Gupta, Sahoo, Chugh, Iota, & Shukla, 2020). If a user uses Facebook as an application, all the responsibilities of the user should be taken by Facebook. Regarding administrative sanction, the Ministry of communication and Informatics will take cares and while criminal activities are of concern, the police will take care.

7.3 VIOLATING OF RIGHTS TO PRIVACY (SINGAPORE CASE RELATED TO FACEBOOK)

Recently, more than 80,000 Facebook users in Singapore face the data theft by the third party. The protection of personal data commission (PDPC) says they are watching closely any contact with Facebook regarding this issue. PDPC is concerned that all the users are affected by data-theft approach by the third party on Facebook platform. For this reason, the Cambridge Analytics opened an office to monitor the same in Singapore. Day by day, many such threats are detected by Cambridge analytics. But all these issues related to Singapore's Defence and academy is not solved.

The leading company called TRIO academics access to Facebook data collected in the same way that Cambridge Analytics did. But after accessing the information, they used that information for other purposes. Also, Nigel Oakes's first company called BDI (Behavioural Dynamic Institute) has linked with Singapore defence academy to protect the content from unauthorised access. As a discussion between Ministry of Defence, Ministry of Home Affairs, and the prime minister of Singapore related to the data access pattern in Facebook (Sahoo & Gupta, 2020). After the concern about security by the Singapore Government, the people of Singapore say that they could not boycott Facebook totally but are more aware about sharing any content and communicating with people.

7.4 DATA PROTECTION BASED ON INTERNATIONAL AND NATIONAL LAW

The protection of user's privacy laws in Indonesia cannot be separated from general guidelines of international legal instrument itself. The National law in Indonesia is influenced based on international laws such as Pancasila as the Constitution of the Republic of Indonesia constructed on 1945. To implement the International rules the following will be conveyed on the action and the international developments.

7.4.1 International Law Instrument–Based Evolution of Protection of Privacy Rights

The fundamental rights called protection of privacy by the law and international conventions. After the World War II, the protection of privacy rights was documented by international law followed by the establishment of UN (United Nation) that replaced the society of nation. One of the professors of public law and Government Emirates, Alan F Westin, divides privacy development in to different phases mention below.

- *The first privacy baseline*: After World War II, people trust the government and different business sectors to gather personal information. At that time people were not bothered about the access of public information. The information was collected for the development of standardisation and benefit of population.

- *The first era of contemporary privacy development*: This era starts with the technology for data search and used by government and private sectors. To store the data primarily, in 1960, the third-generation technology was used by the government sector banks. The personal information of the employee and users are stored by the government.
- *The second era of privacy*: At this era, people use video display terminal called VDT and personal computer called PC as an easier way for collecting public information within budget. Internationally, different countries are beginning to develop different guidelines to protect personal data of the users.
- *Third era of privacy*: At this era, privacy has become the main issue for companies and individuals also. This era is also called advancement of Telecommunication technology informatics and media. As the information can be accessed and collected by everyone, this period is also called the globalisation of technology with advancement.

After the development of UN (United Nation) in 1945, the right to privacy are governed with different international instruments mentioned next:

- *UDHR (Universal Declaration of Human Rights)*: This right was established in the year 1948 and presented in Article 12. It stated 'No one shall be subject to arbitrary interference with his privacy, family, home or correspondence, nor to attack upon his honors and reputation.' Every person has the right to protection of the law again any kind of attack. It is the most important instrument because it has been successfully deployed and implemented.
- *ICCPR (International Covenant on Civil and Political Rights)*: It was established in the year 1966 and presented in Article 17 Paragraph (1). It states that no one can interference with the privacy of others, family, home, or correspondence. Also, it is stated that everyone has the right to protect the law against such malicious activities or attacks.

7.5 CONCLUSION

In this chapter, we have presented various scenarios of cyberattack and their legal action in different countries. Nevertheless, this chapter described the behaviour of attacks and their jurisdiction. To protect user information and account content, there is a requirement of government involvement in every step with proper rules and regulation. This section also described various laws imposed in Indonesia to protect user's information from different attacks like data theft and all. In addition, it presents the right to privacy rules to protect user information from unauthorised access.

REFERENCES

Antara, Data Bocor, Elsam: Menutup Facebook Bukan Solusi Tempo. (2018). https:// bisnis.tempo.co/read/1078332/data-bocor-elsam-closing-facebook-not-solution, (accessed May 26, 2018).

Asih Antika, Tahukah Kamu, Kapan Internet Pertama Kali Masuk Ke Indonesia, Official website of Dewan Teknologi Informasi dan Komunikasi Nasional (WANTIKNAS). (2016). http://www.wantiknas.go.id/2016/10/03/tahukahkamu-kapan-internet-pertama-kalimasuk-ke-indonesia/, (accessed May 17, 2018).

Ayuwuragil, K., & Kronologi Pembobolan Facebook oleh Cambridge Analytica, C. N. N. Indonesia (2018). https://www.cnnindonesia.com/teknologi/20180322194919-185-285163/kronologi-pembobol-facebook-oleh-cambridge-analytica, (accessed June 10, 2018).

Dahiya, A., & Gupta, B. B. (2020). An economic incentive-based risk transfer approach for defending against DDoS attacks. *International Journal of E-Services and Mobile Applications (IJESMA)*, *12*(3), 60–84.

Gupta, B. B., Sahoo, S. R., Chugh, P., Iota, V., & Shukla, A. (2020). Defending multimedia content embedded in online social networks (OSNs) using digital watermarking. In *Handbook of research on multimedia cyber security* (pp. 90–113). IGI Global.

Prosser, William as quoted in DeCew, Judith, Privacy, *The stanford encyclopedia of philosophy* (Fall 2012 Eds), Edward N Zalta (Ed.). Can be downloaded at http:// plato.stanford.edu/archives/fall2012/entries/privacy/.

Sahoo, S. R., & Gupta, B. B (2020). Real-time detection of fake account in twitter using machine-learning approach. In *Advances in computational intelligence and communication technology* (pp. 149–159). Springer, Singapore.

Sahoo, S. R., & Gupta, B. B. (2020). Classification of spammer and nonspammer content in online social network using genetic algorithm-based feature selection. *Enterprise Information Systems*, *14*(5), 710–736.

Yusuf, O., Data 1 Juta Pengguna Facebook Indonesia Dicuri, Kompas. (2018). https:// tekno.kompas.com/read/2018/04/05/10133697/data-1-juta-user-facebook-indonesiadicuri, (accessed June 12, 2018).

(2018). Quoted from http://www.australiaplus.com/indonesian/berita/fb-indonesia-dibareskrim/9674954, (accessed May 26).

Index

A

Adversaries, 2, 8, 32
Airbnb, 10
Amazon, 10, 73
Artificial Intelligence (AI), 80, 99
Anonymous Social Media (ASM), 9
Authenticity, 4, 32, 33
AVG privacy fix, 30

B

Blogging, 10, 13, 58
Bookmarking, 10
    Content Sharing, 10
Breach, 15
Broadcast, 12, 15, 24

C

CAPTCHA, 28
    One-time password (OTP), 28
Communication, 1, 5
Consumer review network (CRN), 10
COLOR+, 32
COMPA, 37
    Behavioural Feature based
        analysis, 37
Corporate Espionage, 26
Cross Site Request Forgery
        (CSRF), 42
Crowd re-tweeting, 31
    Content based features, 31
Cyber Security, 71, 78
    Encryption tools, 79
    Network defence wireless tools, 79
    Network security monitoring
        tools, 79
    Packet sniffer, 79
Cyber Attacks, 21
    Advanced Persistent thread, 21
    Classical threats, 24
    Social threats, 26

Cyber Crime, 9
Cyber criminal, 72, 75

D

Data Mining, 55
DDoS, 23
De-anonymization, 39
DeepScan, 31
Deep Learning, 40
Decision recommendation system (DRS), 35
Discussion forum, 10
DRIP, 32

F

Fake profile, 2, 8, 22,
Facebook privacy scanner, 31
flyByNight architecture, 34
    Public key encryption, 34
Friend in middle attacks, 24
Friend or foes, 34
    Dishonest recommendation, 34

G

Google+, 1, 2, 7
Graph based attack, 23

H

Hybrid trust evaluation approach
        (HT–TRUST), 33
    e-commerce, 10, 33

I

Illation attacks, 24
Instagram, 6, 7,

K

Koobface, 21, 25

L

Long short-term memory (LSTM), 31

M

Machine Learning, 31, 32, 36
    COMPA, 37
    Facebook Inspector, 36
    Fake Spotter, 37
Malicious Application, 37
Malwares, 8, 25,83
Malicious URLs, 26, 59
McAfee social security protection, 30
Multiparty Access Control (MPAC), 33

N

Net Nanny, 30
Norton Safe Web (NSW), 30

O

Online Social Network (OSN), 1, 4, 10
Online chat risk, 23
Online predators, 26, 28
OSN aggregator, 25

P

P2P-based key agreement, 32
Persona, 36
Petrinet, 60
Phishing attacks, 21, 25,
Plug-in attack, 24

R

Ransomware, 25
RDF (Resource description
          approach), 35
ReDS, 35

S

Secret Interest Groups (SIGs), 35
Spamming attacks, 25
Spear Phishing, 79
Speculation attack, 23
Sybil attack, 24

T

Temple-based spam detector in OSN
          (Tangram), 33

U

U-control approach, 34

V

Vicinity attack, 23

W

Whaling attack, 21

X

XSS Attack, 30